You can do this!
— Grace

the birds still sing

◆ FriesenPress

Suite 300 - 990 Fort St
Victoria, BC, V8V 3K2
Canada

www.friesenpress.com

Copyright © 2019 by Grace Tallman
Corinne Garlick, Illustrator
First Edition — 2019

All rights reserved.

No part of this publication may be reproduced in any form, or by any means, electronic or mechanical, including photocopying, recording, or any information browsing, storage, or retrieval system, without permission in writing from FriesenPress.

ISBN
978-1-5255-4114-8 (Hardcover)
978-1-5255-4115-5 (Paperback)
978-1-5255-4116-2 (eBook)

1. FAMILY & RELATIONSHIPS, PARENTING, MOTHERHOOD

Distributed to the trade by The Ingram Book Company

Table of Contents

Part One: The Journey Begins 1

    Childbirth 3

    My Dad 9

    School Days 16

    My Mother 21

    Bruce 32

    Our Marriage 39

    Hospital Chaplaincy Training 48

    Positive Pregnancy Test 52

    At Home with My New Baby 58

    Rock Bottom 63

    Return to Darkness 68

Getting Help 73

My Brother Henry.. 76

Life on the Psychiatric Ward...................................... 82

The Road to Recovery 87

Epilogue 91

Part Two: Paths To Resilience 101

What is Resilience?.. 103

A. *Principles Of Resilience*....................................... 106

B. *Steps To Building Resilience* 112

Part Three: Some Specific Suggestions For Prevention and Care of Postpartum Depression 131

1. *Education and Awareness* 133

2. *Funding for Public Health Home Visits*.......................... 134

3. *Know the Risk Factors*.. 134

4. *Recognize the Existing Social Stigma* 135

5. *Medical Follow-up*.. 135

6. *Friends and Partners Can Help*.................... 136

Acknowledgements.. 139

"Hope" is the thing with feathers
That perches in the soul
And sings the tune without the words
And never stops—at all.

—Emily Dickinson

the birds still sing

My Journey of Resilience
Through Postpartum Depression

My own personal experience with postpartum depression is the impetus for this book. If sharing my story helps even one woman avoid this potentially life-threatening experience, I will have succeeded in a significant way.

PART ONE:
The Journey Begins

Childbirth

And something inside me just broke...
that's the only way I could describe it.
—Ranata Suzuki

I should've been happy—very, very happy. Even ecstatic. I had just given birth to the most perfect, beautiful little girl. Her skin was a healthy pink, her face scrunched up, and her eyes still closed. She had a soft tuft of dark hair on top of her tiny head. She had ten miniature fingers and toes. I counted them; they were all there. Her hands were curled in tiny tight fists that she waved in front of her unseeing eyes. What a shock it must have been for her to have emerged from a dark, warm place of safety into a world that was unknown and scary. She weighed six pounds, thirteen ounces. She was absolutely flawless! I clutched her little body against me. We snuggled, skin to skin.

Part of me took in the beautiful little baby and I held her in my arms. My love for her was immediate. I was flooded with waves of gratitude and relief. Wearily, I hugged her tightly and held her to my breast. Instinctively, she suckled vigorously as we established our mother-daughter bond. Her instincts guided her. She knew what to do; nobody had to show or teach her.

But another part of me realized that even though I wanted to hold her forever, I did not have the strength to do it for more than a few minutes.

The nurses wrapped her in a warm, pink-striped flannel blanket and placed a knitted stocking cap on her head to keep her warm and cozy. She was wheeled to the nursery in her little bassinet for continued observation. The initial assessment indicated that her Apgar score was a perfect ten out of ten. The Apgar test is a quick assessment that is performed on all infants at birth. The newborns are rated on skin colour, muscle tone, breathing, movement, and, of course, their ability to make that first, lusty cry.

I was taken to another room for a brief recuperation and to await discharge from the hospital. I was completely alone. I lay down in my bed and curled up in a fetal position and turned toward the wall. I was physically and emotionally exhausted. My body was wracked with silent sobs. Inexplicable, bewildering sadness sliced my heart. Tears soaked the crisp white hospital sheets. I drew the curtain around my bed to shut out the world. Darkness enveloped my being. The world turned black. I had been robbed of the joy that should have permeated this momentous event.

Silently and angrily, I cried out to God. "You gave me this untimely, unexpected pregnancy. Surely you could have given me an easier labour. You could have protected me from going back into this familiar dark emptiness of depression and despair. Where are you, God? I feel so alone, cut off from all hope and meaning."

❦

My husband, Bruce, had driven me to the hospital at around 8:00 p.m., the evening before. I was a day past my due date. I was having irregular contractions that refused to evolve into active labour. Bruce had taken the day off to be with me in case my labour progressed. We'd spent the afternoon walking around Gibbons Park with the hopes that the movement would bring on my labour. It was a hot day for early May. My large belly added to the uncomfortable warmth I felt. I would not complain; we had waited a long time for the weather to warm up. Hundreds of Canada geese waddled around the park in tight pairs. The ganders honked and hissed protectively when anyone approached them, while the females sat patiently on their eggs. This mating was serious business! Bruce and I fit right in with these feathered creatures. We were all waiting for new life to enter the world.

When we'd arrived at the hospital, the nurses had hooked me up to an IV and started an oxytocin drip to stimulate the labour. Within minutes, the contractions had come on like bulldozers and the pain had become unbearable.

I had every intention of going the natural route this time. I had done this twice before, and this time I wanted to do it right. I told Bruce that I did not want an epidural. That was then. This was now. Before long, I was begging for pain relief. My body tensed up with each wave of pain. I was doing the exact opposite of what I had been trained to do in my Lamaze classes. I had been taught to ride each contraction with rhythmic breathing and to distract myself from the pain by gazing at a focal point on the wall in front of me. The only thing I was able to focus on was the excruciating tightening of my belly as the contractions keep rolling along in unstoppable succession.

The nurses called for an anesthetist, who placed a tiny plastic catheter next to my spinal cord. He injected an anesthetic and, within seconds, I was completely numb from the waist down. Relief! One of the nurses did an internal exam to check my progress. She told me that I would be ready to start pushing within minutes. It was almost over!

By this time, I had been awake the entire night and in active labour for nine hours. I was exhausted! Bruce was angry. He was supposed to make sure that my wishes were adhered to and this was definitely not what I had expressed to him. Bruce got into a verbal altercation with the nurses about the epidural. "Why didn't you check her progress before calling the anesthetist? She didn't want an epidural." He was my protector and wanted to honour my intention to have this baby naturally. He was certain that if I had known I was as close as I was to the end of my labour, I could have endured.

But by this point I no longer cared. I was so relieved to be out of pain, nothing else mattered. The nurses were taken aback by Bruce's outburst. They left the room and never returned.

That was when I hit a major problem. I was being told to push with each contraction, but was completely numb. I had no idea when I was having a contraction. The nurses had abandoned me. Poor Bruce felt absolutely helpless and hovered over me anxiously.

Because I could not feel my abdominal muscles, I was unable to push effectively. My face was flushed and sweat was pouring off my body. Bruce dabbed a cool washcloth on my face in an effort to soothe me. My neck muscles felt like knotted ropes. My eyes felt like they were going to pop out of their sockets.

The doctor told me to push harder and I wanted to scream: "I can't push any harder. I'm trying my very best!" But I didn't have the energy to respond.

This final stage of labour normally lasts about thirty minutes, but I had been pushing for three hours. I collapsed with absolute exhaustion. "I can't go on," I whispered through cracked lips. The doctor put his face a few inches from mine, and in a stern voice, commanded me to keep going. I will never forget his words: "**YES, YOU CAN**," he shouted.

Somehow, I gathered my strength, and with every ounce of remaining energy, gave a final push. The doctor caught the slippery little body and announced triumphantly, "It's a girl!" I think he was as relieved as I was. I could tell he had been getting worried.

Sighs of relief and triumph filled the room. My mind barely registered what was going on around me, but somewhere, as if from a far distance, I heard the unmistakable cry of a newborn. Finally, my struggle was over. I crumpled against the bed in utter weariness.

Back in my hospital room, I was in a state of complete mental and physical fatigue. A nurse showed up with a tray of lunch: a cellophane-wrapped sandwich and a somewhat wilted salad of lettuce and tomatoes. I had no interest in eating. In their eagerness to get us discharged, not one nurse or doctor asked me how I was doing. I felt completely overwhelmed and unprepared to go home and take care of a newborn baby. I didn't even know if I could take care of myself.

I don't know how much time elapsed, but another nurse eventually brought in my beautiful baby girl. We had decided that, if it was a girl, we would name her Alana. The nurse briskly announced that we were ready to go home. Somehow, I mustered the strength to dress Alana in the little yellow onesie I'd brought to the hospital in my suitcase. I secured her in her car seat and we were wheeled to the front door of the hospital where Bruce was waiting in the car.

It was a beautiful May morning. Golden forsythia bushes exploded around the hospital, the birds sang cheerful songs, the sky was a cloudless blue. This form of natural beauty usually filled me with awe and elation, but on this day, none of these wonders lessened the exhaustion and darkness that had taken over my mind.

My Dad

Nobody ever drowned in his own sweat
—Ann Landers

If you were to visit the farm where I grew up, you would see a cluster of granaries, a long, low-slung barn for the dairy cattle and pigs, and a fenced-in outdoor pen made of rough pine logs for the beef cattle. Squatting in the centre would be a large gravel yard, dominated by a lofty two-storey house.

Our farm was surrounded by clumps of poplar trees that sheltered us from the passing cars and pickup trucks that rumbled by on the dusty road. Saskatoon bushes that bore luscious berries in early summer were scattered amidst the trees around the edges of our yard. The land for miles around is flat as a pig's snout, with gravel roads that intersect on a perfect grid.

Our nearest neighbours lived about a quarter of a mile to the west. They owned a large dairy farm, and I often walked there to buy milk in a two-litre, ice-cream pail. I left the payment for my purchase in a basket on the windowsill. The honour system worked well in our small farming community.

Growing up in a family with eleven children seemed normal to me; I didn't think it was at all unusual. In our community, large families were the norm. The more children, the more helping hands to run the farm and tend to household chores.

Life on the farm was no picnic. Expectations for hard work around the home and farm were set at a high bar. Slacking off was seen as a cardinal sin. There was no shortage of work in any season. There was one rule: No play was allowed until the work was done.

When the long winter months finally relented and the last drifts of snow had melted away, Dad would bring out his rototiller and turned over the rich Manitoba gumbo in the gardens that surrounded our house. I would inhale the earthy smell of freshly cultivated soil. This was a sure sign of spring. It was also the signal for the backbreaking toil of starting the garden for another season.

The garden duties fell on Mom and her three daughters. Seeding rows and rows of potatoes, corn, peas, and beans was just the start. Once the plants peeked through the black soil, the weeds followed. I recall hours and hours of hoeing the garden until my hands were blistered and my back ached. I longed to join my cousin at the Sandpit for a cool, refreshing swim, but until every weed had been banished, I knew there was no point in begging to go.

What we produced in the garden was our source of food for the winter months. "If you don't work, you don't eat," was my father's mantra. On blistering summer days, the five youngest siblings would congregate on the lawn in the shade of the oak tree, each of us balancing a bowl on our lap for the peas that we were shelling. If it wasn't peas, it was cutting up beans, or stuffing cucumbers into jars with long stems of dill, for pickles. We canned and froze enough vegetables to feed a small army. The pantry shelves in our basement were lined with a rainbow of colours: green beans, red beets, yellow peaches, dill pickles, relishes, and jams. A huge bin in a dark corner of the basement was filled with potatoes. We preserved carrots in sawdust. The giant freezer was full of homegrown chicken, pork, and beef.

Every winter, members of my mother's family came over for pig-butchering day. I remember covering my ears at the pig's horrible shriek when my dad cut its throat. I was filled with revulsion at the thought of what was happening in the barn and relieved that I didn't have to witness the actual act of killing, which was done behind closed barn doors. I made sure to stay away as far as possible, but the sound of the dying pig lingered in my mind for days.

Next, my mother's parents, three of her brothers, and their wives would converge on our farmyard for a day of intense labour. They would hover all day over a huge cauldron in our basement, extracting every possible tidbit of edible meat from the pig. My stomach would turn at the sight of pickled pigs' feet in large mason jars. Other equally disgusting-looking and -tasting remnants were preserved and stored for the months ahead.

What my dad lacked in physical height he more than made up for with his larger-than-life personality. He was vivacious, garrulous, and thoroughly extroverted. He laughed heartily at his own jokes while the rest of us groaned. He was an enthusiastic optimist, and usually looked on the brighter side of life. He had a habit of whistling as he worked. I recall feeling happy at this cheery sound. He could run circles around many of his counterparts with his energy and hard work. He loved his children with an unspoken affection.

After a hard day's work on the farm, he would challenge the rest of the family to a rousing game of baseball or football. That was another fringe benefit of such a large family: we had enough members to form a small team for whatever sport we engaged in. His energy and enthusiasm were unsurpassed. His competitive nature was evident in everything he did, including the physical games we played together.

Dad was a staunch supporter of the local church and he spoke openly and fervently about his Christian beliefs. His faith in God demanded harsh adherence to strict, black-and-white moral principles. He strongly believed that it was his duty as a father to ensure that his children followed these teachings without questioning. Dad possessed a fiery temper that often took the form of harsh punishment. His rules and expectations could not be breached. His goal was to raise a family of God-fearing children, and his methodology was basically to beat any rebellious attitudes out of us with severe whippings. He used a worn leather strap, which he wielded in his powerful hands. His intent was to inflict enough pain to break our spirits.

The Birds Still Sing

I will never forget the beating I received when I was fourteen. I was at the height of individuating as an adolescent. I rebelled at being the submissive person my dad was trying to force me to be. I was asking bold, existential questions: "Who am I as an individual? Who am I apart from being a member of this large family? What is my personality? What are my own values? What do I want to do with my life?"

This boundary-pushing was a totally normal rite of passage. I had had enough of being held captive by a controlling father. One night, I ignored my eleven o'clock curfew and stayed out with my friends. We had a wonderful time engaging in normal teenage behaviour. We found a clearing in a nearby woodlot where we spent a carefree time just hanging out. We enjoyed each other's company, laughing, drinking beer, smoking, listening to music: normal teenage stuff; nothing dangerous or evil.

We completely lost track of time as we gave over to the enjoyment of the moment. It must have been around 2:00 a.m. when one of my friends finally drove me home. The minute I walked into the house, I knew things were not going to be OK. My dad greeted me with a scowl on his face. "Where have you been? You know you're supposed to be home by eleven." The leather strap dangled from his hand. He ordered me to strip off my jeans and for the next twenty minutes, he proceeded to lash my bare buttocks with the leather strap, swinging his strong arms with all the strength he could manage. Red hot pain seared my tender flesh. I fought to shield the pain with my arms. Throughout this ruthless beating, I glimpsed my mother standing helplessly nearby, dressed in her white flannel nightgown, tears streaming down her face. She made no effort to protect me. Perhaps she felt I had brought this upon myself, or perhaps she knew that he would have turned on her if she had intervened.

Sleep eluded me that night. Waves of confused thoughts rushed through my mind. How could a father do this to his own daughter? Why did my mother not invoke her maternal instincts to protect me from this violence? The next morning, I got up in a daze. My arms and legs were covered with angry purple welts and bruises that proclaimed the awful events of the previous night. I wandered into the woods behind our barn. I walked until I was a long way from our house. That's when I started sobbing, silently at first and then with increasing abandon. I released my emotions in a torrent of anguish, yielding to my emotional pain with plaintive cries. The silent trees opened their arms in voiceless comfort. The birds still sang as they darted from branch to branch.

Their songs connected me to the goodness of the earth, the ageless affirming fortress of unchanging strength beneath me. I knew that what my father did to me had been wrong, wrong, WRONG. I felt no love behind the harsh punishment, only anger and vengeance. My father was losing his strong grip on me, and he was unable to tolerate not being in full control. The thinly disguised explanation that he wanted what was best for me made absolutely no sense to me. I resented the religious fanaticism, quoting Bible verses that he used to justify his actions. I vowed that he would never do this to me again. EVER!

My father mellowed greatly over the ensuing years. The harshness that characterized his earlier years was increasingly replaced by loving concern and support. He became more affectionate and started telling his children that he loved them, words I had never encountered in my growing-up years.

The forcefulness that he demonstrated in his younger years had, after all, been the product of his own harsh upbringing. The stress of providing for a large family on a meagre income of a struggling farm created significant pressure. This stress was compounded by the rebellious teen years of his growing children. I am afraid that we became the target of some of the intolerable burden he carried.

After leaving the toil of the farm, he retired and led a more leisurely lifestyle. Following my mother's death, he married a widow who lived in the local community. Matilda proved to be a vibrant, loving companion to him in his old age. He died at the ripe age of ninety-nine years. At his funeral a few years ago, he was extolled by his many grandchildren through loving tributes. I know that his example influenced me to become a hard worker, and to develop a strong sense of ethics and morals, and an unflinching "can-do" attitude toward life's many challenges.

Although Dad never acknowledged the harsh treatment he inflicted on me, I have forgiven him. He had a hard, unrelenting life, and under the circumstances, he did the best that any father could have done.

School Days

Nothing makes us so lonely as our secrets.
—Paul Tournier

The school in our farming community was located exactly one mile east of our farm. Every morning, I walked the distance along the gravel road. It didn't matter what the weather was like, whether it was minus thirty or pouring rain, I was expected to find my way to and from school. I usually found one or more of the other neighbourhood children to walk with. There were no school buses and my dad didn't believe in spoiling his children by driving them. He told us many stories of how he walked a long distance to school when he was young, and he didn't have much sympathy for any whining about having to walk.

There were two rooms in our school. Room One housed the younger children, from grades one to four. The lower grades were taught by a young female teacher who did her best to keep the boisterous farm children under control. Room Two was where the older children were taught. As a young child, I longed to be in the second classroom with the more grown-up children who seemed to be so mature and self-confident. The school served a small farming community and the student body had no more than fifty students at any given time.

The school was surrounded by grassy fields, with four baseball diamonds and several soccer fields. In the early fall and spring, we played baseball. In the colder months, we played soccer. All the students were expected to play outside at recess time. We had no indoor gymnasium. I'm sure the teachers sighed with relief when the students retreated to the outdoors. You had to have a pretty convincing excuse to be allowed to stay inside. I think the pedagogy behind this was to try and diffuse any extraneous bottled-up energy that accumulated from sitting at a desk for several hours throughout the day.

In the months of May and June, track and field events became part of our recreational curriculum. Students expended a great deal of energy in their efforts to scale the high jump bar, trying to break their personal bests. Everybody had an opportunity to try and excel in the individual events they were good at: broad jump, pole vaulting, sprints, dashes, and cross-country races. The ultimate goal was to compete at the annual school picnic and go home with a winning red ribbon.

The school picnic was the social event of the year. Farmers took the day off and gathered at the schoolyard to take part in the festivities of the day that marked the end of the school year. Families packed picnic lunches and spread out on blankets under the shade of the trees that bordered the schoolyard. A makeshift store was set up in the garage of the teacherage. You could buy a bottle of cold pop for ten cents and a chocolate bar for five cents.

The time finally arrived when I graduated into Room Two. I was so proud to be promoted to the fifth grade. I felt like I had arrived. I was a bright student, and always competed for first place in my class. Now I had even more opportunities to learn. I eavesdropped on the lessons being taught to the grade seven and eight students, and by the time I got to the higher grades, I felt like I was reviewing material I had already learned.

There were a lot of adjustments that I had to make as I became part of the older classroom. I had always admired the teachers in my earlier years. They were strict but had a gentle, maternal manner that made me comfortable. I wasn't quite sure how I would adapt to being in a classroom with a male teacher.

Mr. W. seemed to take a rather uncanny interest in me. He made some very personal comments to me about my developing body. It made me feel like crawling under my desk. I was aware enough to realize that what he was saying was inappropriate, but I had no idea how to handle this unwanted attention. I began to feel ashamed and self-conscious about my body. I had been perfectly happy with my body as a child and would have much preferred it to stay that way. I was somewhat mystified by the changes that were happening to me as I began entering early puberty. I felt awkward and embarrassed at having these changes noticed and commented on, especially by my teacher!

As the months passed by, Mr. W. became bolder in his comments and gradually started seeking out opportunities to find me alone. To my horror, he began touching parts of my body in ways that I knew were improper and perverse. Day after day, he found excuses to find me when no one else was around and continued to fixate his attention on me. I had no way of escaping. I was trapped. I was confused. I felt consumed with guilt. What had I done to attract this attention? I believed that it must be my fault, that I must be doing something sinful to cause his behaviour.

It was my dirty little secret. I had to make sure that nobody ever found out what was happening to me. There was no one in whom I could confide. If I told my friends or sisters, they would only confirm my deepest fears that I was bringing this on myself, that I was to blame. I couldn't fathom telling my parents. My dad made it perfectly clear that authority in any form was never to be challenged. Unquestioning obedience was the only course of action of which he approved. As my teacher, Mr. W. was a highly respected authority figure. Even if I had dared tell my dad, not only would he have not believed me, he would have punished me severely.

I locked up my secret in the darkest, remotest corner of my brain. It was a place like the attic in our house. The trap door to it was in the ceiling just outside my bedroom. It was only on the rarest of occasions that anyone ventured up there. Once I was brave enough to climb up and look around just to satisfy my curiosity. Cobwebs draped eerily from the sloped rafters. It was as dark as midnight. Without a flashlight, it would have been impossible to see the few boxes that someone had stored up there.

I tried to pretend that my life was normal. At school, I continued to do well academically and interacted with my classmates. At home, I became more and more isolated, seeking refuge in the woods behind our farm when I found an opportunity to slip away from my chores. Here I found refuge from the fear that I would be found out. There was no one to bother me here, no one to ask unwanted questions; there was no way that my secret would be found out.

My Mother

Mother is the name for
God in the lips and hearts of little children.
—William Makepeace Thackeray

My mother had soft blue eyes and dark brown hair that she kept fastened in a neat bun at the nape of her neck. I remember watching in fascination as she wound her long dark hair and secured it in place with four large bobby pins. She wore simple, cotton print dresses and an apron tied around a waist that was thickened with her repeated childbearing.

In sharp contrast to my dad's outgoing, exuberant personality, my mother's humility and gentleness were her trademarks. She would do anything to help someone in need. Ironically, she completely lacked the concept of standing up for her own needs. In fact, I doubt that she was even aware that she had the right to have any desires other than serving her family and community.

Mom had an unwavering faith in God. She was loved and respected by everyone who knew her. Many people in the community approached her for advice or comfort when they were facing tough challenges. Her upbringing demanded that her husband's needs and wants be paramount. She was, indeed, the biblical, submissive, and obedient wife. Looking back, I now realize that this was why she was unable to protect me from my dad's harshness. She was caught in the impossible dilemma of choosing between a strict code of obedience to her husband and a role of motherly protection. I recognized that agonized look of quandary on her face the night I suffered that unforgettable beating.

I cannot say that she resented her lot in life, because she never complained. Any anger or bitterness she may have experienced was not demonstrated outwardly. She held all of this deep inside her, and I sometimes wonder if this may have been the cause of a deep melancholy that often seemed to overshadow her.

My mother held an unquestioning faith in the God of her forefathers. She clung to her beliefs like a life raft through the darkness and harsh realities of her life. Even as a young child, the mournful hymns she sang wrapped my heart in sadness. Bone-weary, she willed her body to prepare another meal for her hungry family. In the midst of playing with my dolls upstairs, I would pause to listen to her quiet, mournful voice in the kitchen below me. Her sadness penetrated me as if it were my own. Perhaps she thought the singing would boost her sagging spirits and imbue her with the strength and energy she needed to get through another day of endless toil. Looking back, I now know she was struggling with feelings of deep depression. In those days, there was no language to express that kind of burden.

She loved all eleven children equally, and her grandchildren were her pride and joy. I don't know how she endured eleven pregnancies, plus two more babies that didn't survive. There was always an undertone of grief when she talked about the baby girl who was born with the umbilical cord wrapped around her neck.

Childbirth took place in the home during those days. Most women could survive with the help of a self-taught midwife. But this case was different. The doctor was called, but he got there too late and didn't have the necessary skills to deal with this high-risk situation. The loss of a perfectly formed, full-term child is a heartache that carves a permanent hole in the heart of the mother who carried her next to her breast for nine months.

Of course, childbirth in a close-knit community was an event that was shared by all of its women. There was a sisterhood that understood the struggles that accompanied the childrearing years. No woman ever suffered these hardships alone. There were meals and fresh loaves of bread sent during the first weeks of recovery.

Women spent a whole month in bed after giving birth. It was common practice to hire a mother's helper to look after the chores of the household, as well as to care for other young children. This was considered excellent training and preparation for the neighbourhood teenage girls who filled this role. The only expectation of them was that one day they would be married and have children of their own. What better way to learn and get the training.

My mother instilled a love of books and reading in us at an early age. Bedtime was story time. Three or four of the youngest children would gather around her; the older ones would lean over her shoulder and the smaller ones would clamber onto her lap. Her stories, of course, included all the fascinating heroes from the Bible, but she also read us tales from a series of children's books called Uncle Arthur's *Bedtime Stories*. Most of these stories included some form of moral truths or lessons. I also remember listening to her reading from John Bunyan's *The Pilgrim's Progress*. I must admit that my preschool level of comprehension missed the finer truths of this metaphorical tale. We would beg for "just one more story" each time she closed a book and shooed us off to bed. "OK, just one more short story," she would eventually relent.

My mother helped me fill out my first order form to request books to be sent by mail from the University of Manitoba. Every other week, I would receive a neatly wrapped cardboard package in our mailbox with four or five books. I would promptly devour them and pore over the catalogue eagerly, making selections for my next order. There were always shelves of books in our house. My brothers had the entire collection of Hardy Boy mystery books. I collected the Nancy Drew series. There was no end to enthralling stories to read: *Black Beauty, Tom Sawyer, Huckleberry Finn*. As soon as I completed my chores, I became lost in the world of make-believe between the covers of a book. In this way, I visited faraway places and learned about the world beyond the little community I lived in.

When I do the calculations, I realize that my mother was pregnant for approximately twelve years of her life. Many of these pregnancies were fraught with anxiety and risk. At the age of thirty-seven, when she was pregnant with her ninth child, she developed excruciating abdominal pain. The pain was relentless and unbearable. When she arrived at the hospital, she was rushed to the operating room where the doctors discovered a large, cancerous ovarian tumour pressing on her lower abdomen. Because she was pregnant, the treatment was very conservative. The doctors removed the tumour and sent my mother home to wait out the remainder of her pregnancy. She miraculously delivered a healthy baby boy, my little brother, Lauren. Little did she realize that this cancer would become a life sentence—a ball and chain that she would, in some form, drag with her for the rest of her life.

Sooner or later, an untreated malignant tumour would return to rear its ugly head again. I don't remember my exact age, but I think I was ten or eleven when we received the devastating news that Mom's cancer had returned. A dark, heavy cloud saturated with the possibility that she might die hung over our heads. That night, my two sisters Hilda and Catherine and I huddled in our upstairs bedroom. A sloping ceiling followed the angle of the roof, lending a cozy atmosphere to the tiny room the three of us shared. A bright patchwork quilt on the double bed lent some cheerful colour to the plain, sparse room. A sheer organza curtain drifted in the breeze of our east-facing window. Outside the partly open window, robins sang their cheery nesting songs, oblivious to the sadness that had invaded our young lives. We knelt on a homemade braided rug beside the bed and prayed in desperation for our mother's return to health. We were filled with grief and uncertainty. What would we do if our mother died? I couldn't visualize a life without her loving presence. The very word "cancer" filled us with dread. We had heard many whispered adult conversations about people who died of cancer. Was our mother to be the next?

I lived in a daze for the next few weeks. I made my way to school each day as usual. My heart was leaden. I could not engage in the usual banter with the neighbourhood children. Mr. W. and the entire community were aware of the heartache that our family was experiencing. It seemed that, in his distorted way of thinking, he thought he would bring comfort to me by continuing to single me out with his inappropriate touching. The dark, guarded corner of my brain was becoming chock-full with all the sadness and shame I was trying to ignore so that I could carry on with my life. I found that I could not concentrate or focus on Canadian history, arithmetic, or book reports. I was filled with unspeakable sadness. Life just wasn't the same without my mother at home. My mind was with my mother as I visualized her confined to a hospital bed, her future grim and uncertain.

The prognosis became a little less sombre as time passed. The doctor prescribed a course of radiation. Mom went for her treatments every week day for a period of time. It seems to me it was something like six weeks. This meant driving the one-hour trip to the St. Boniface Hospital in Winnipeg, where the treatments took place. The trips to Winnipeg were a perfect alternative to the regular routine I was so accustomed to. The warm spring weather contributed to the exciting adventure of the little getaways. With her newly minted driver's licence my older sister Hilda got ample practice behind the wheel. She acted as the chauffeur, and the younger siblings got their turns to go along for the ride. My poor mother's ailing health was almost forgotten in the excitement of stops at McDonald's for burgers, fries, and milkshakes on our way home.

The radiation must have been successful because Mom regained her health and became just "Mom" again. Soon, she was back to baking her Saturday-morning batches of bread and buns, which would last her large family for the coming week. I can still see her bent over the huge pans as she kneaded the dough until it was smooth and satiny. Soon, the aroma of fresh bread would waft through the house. Even to this day, I think of my mother when I smell bread baking.

When she was given a clean bill of health five years later, we all cheered and assumed that she was going to be around for a long time. For the time being, the threat of losing her was behind us.

Mom had about an eighteen-year reprieve this time, long enough for all of us to think that she had finally beaten the illness once and for all. But the virility of malignant cells cannot be underestimated. There must have been some renegade cancer cells lurking in her body that were out of reach of the powerful radiation beams.

By this time, I was married and a young mother living in Winnipeg. I recall in vivid detail receiving the call on the beige rotary phone that hung on my kitchen wall. I clearly see the pale-yellow walls of my kitchen, the shiny linoleum floor. I hear my dad's tear-filled voice on the other end of the line, relaying the devastating message that once again Mom was being rushed into emergency surgery. This time, it was a bowel obstruction. He wasn't sure if she was going to make it. Once more, the family was plunged into sadness and anxiety. We all feared the worst. She did make it through the surgery, but her body was permanently disfigured by a colostomy. The disease with that ugly name, "cancer," had returned.

From that point on, Mom became more fragile. She was never able to accept the colostomy, which caused her many embarrassing and odorous situations in public washrooms. The chemotherapy to which she was subjected left her with severe nausea and vomiting, and she begged the doctors to discontinue it. She just could not bear what it was doing to her weakened body. The doctor responded without empathy and understanding, "Then the cancer will kill you."

Mom felt she had no voice in the decision that was being made for her. Somehow, she soldiered through the course of chemotherapy. The poison that was meant to destroy the cancer cells also attacked her body with brutal force. The invasive treatment had a demoralizing impact on her life—on all of our lives. I can still see her standing tearfully in front of the mirror, holding a handful of her long hair in her hands. Losing her hair was like losing a part of herself. She continued to struggle with weakness and intractable nausea and vomiting. The months that followed were focused on making the best of a very sorrowful situation; buying a suitable wig to conceal a bald head, coping with a leaky colostomy, and coming to grips with increasing pain. By far the worst consequence was the very real possibility that this time the cancer would defeat her in her brave struggle to survive.

I made it a top priority to spend as much time with my mother as I could. On my days off, I bundled our two children, Hailey and Brandon, in the car and drove the hour to the farm. Seeing Mom sitting listlessly on the brown plaid couch in the living room of their house broke my heart. Her hair had grown back, thicker and wavier than before her chemo, but it did not make up for the grey pallor of her skin. One of the things that brought some diversion and cheer to her life at this dismal time was the birdbath that the family bought her. We placed it just outside her kitchen window so that she could watch as the birds splashed happily without a care in the world. The first robin returning in the spring had always filled her with excitement. Her motherly role of cooking meals for her family, doing household chores, and basically taking care of everyone was a distant memory. The tables were turned. Now we were doing what we could to take care of her.

The cancer continued to ravage her failing body. She shrivelled to half her former size. She lost her strength, her appetite, and even her will to live. She merely survived as the relentless pain worsened and her frailty overtook her. One thing she never lost was her love for and devotion to her family, especially her grandchildren. She always had a weak smile and hug for each of them, no matter how she was feeling. Somehow she knew that her life would live on through them into the next generations.

She made a final trip to the hospital. We all knew this was the beginning of the end as she could do nothing more to help herself. The nurses cared for her as well as they could and changed her position every two hours—"to prevent bedsores," they said. The slightest movement triggered unbearable pain and her agonized cries are etched in my mind forever. I begged the nurses to just let her stay in one position, knowing that time was quickly running out for her. She was given a pitifully inadequate dose of morphine in an IV drip. I pleaded with her doctor to increase her pain medication. I was appalled at his response. "She will get addicted." Addicted!! Could he not see that she had only weeks to live?

We took turns keeping a constant loving vigil at her bedside. Her pain was our pain. Our vain efforts did very little to alleviate her suffering. The time had come when instead of praying for her healing, we begged for her to be released from the hell she was enduring.

The call to say that she had died came around 11 p.m., on April 27, 1988. Despite a deep sense of loss, I couldn't help feeling relief and peace, knowing that her agony had ended at last. I am sure that the gates of heaven opened wide to receive a faithful saint. I could almost hear the angels singing as they welcomed her to her eternal home. When I reflected on my mother's last year of life, I realized that I had no regrets. I had spent many precious moments with her during her illness. We communicated and connected with each other in a deeper way than we ever had when she was in good health. About two months before she died, I finally found the courage to disclose Mr. W.'s ongoing sexual abuse throughout the four years while he was my teacher.

"Why didn't you tell me earlier?" she cried. She was incredulous and heartbroken at what I had endured.

"I didn't think I would have been believed," I responded. My mother's tears and her warm hug were proof enough that she believed every word I had told her. Together, we wept. We both realized that it was too late for her to intervene in any way, but I felt that if she had had the opportunity, she would have done anything in her power to vindicate the innocence that had been stolen from me. An unspoken barrier had been dissolved between us, drawing us closer than ever in our mother–daughter relationship. My mother went to her grave carrying my secret with her. I will never regret entrusting her without reservation.

My mother's example would continue to have a strong influence on me for the rest of my life. Her personality, her compassion, and love became a part of who I was. On a subconscious level, I absorbed her self-effacing ways, always putting others ahead of myself, not acknowledging my own needs and desires.

Looking back over time, I now know that if she had lived longer, her heart would have been broken into a million pieces by a tragedy that was to befall our family in the next five years.

Bruce

Being deeply loved by someone gives you strength, while loving someone deeply gives you courage.
—Lao-Tzu

At the age of twenty-four, I settled back into the community where I grew up after attending a Bible college in Vancouver for three years. My teenage years of rebellion were gone and forgotten. I was living with my parents, and we lived harmoniously, for the most part. I accepted their way of life and adopted it as my own. The community around me was a source of rich nurturing and support. Although I was generally content and satisfied with my life, I couldn't help noticing that most of my close friends were getting married. My boyfriend wasn't making any moves toward a serious relationship and I was feeling impatient. I began worrying about becoming an "old maid." In retrospect, I realize that my fears were premature and unrealistic; in fact, completely unfounded. But the feeling nagged at me. I felt like I was missing out on romance. That was when Bruce entered my life.

I worked at a daycare centre for children and adults with developmental delays. Their condition was referred to as mental retardation in those days. This, of course, is no longer a politically correct term. Our daycare was located in a mid-sized town about seven miles from our farming community. We were housed in an old one-storey building that had been a former schoolhouse and suited our purpose perfectly. The centre was staffed by two women besides myself. Greta, our manager, was a stout, kind-hearted woman with staunch Mennonite values. She would do anything in her power to give the best possible care to our clients. My other colleague was an attractive American woman from Wisconsin named Vera. She had married a local man and taken up Canadian citizenship. She was a few years older than me.

The three of us shared a lot of laughter and camaraderie and worked hard as a team to do the best for our clients. We were given basic behaviour-modification training. We used our skills to provide positive reinforcement for desirable behaviours. We doled out countless tiny sweet treats: chocolate chips, Froot Loops, and Smarties the minute we noticed a client doing something that was deemed a positive behaviour. We attempted to put less desirable behaviours on "extinction" by ignoring them.

Our clients were at a low level of functioning, most of them lacking the basic skills to care for themselves. We spent endless hours going through the motions of teaching those skills that we hoped would enhance their living situation.

We broke the different tasks into tiny individual steps so that our clients could learn activities of daily living by rote. The average person performs these skills—such as brushing your teeth, washing your hands and face as well as dressing and undressing—on a daily basis without even pausing to think. One of our clients was not even able to feed himself when he first came to us. With a great deal of patience, the staff persisted, day after day, in placing a thick-handled spoon in his rigid hand and guiding it to his mouth, over and over. The taste of the food in his mouth provided an instant reward, and, within a period of two months, he was eating by himself. We kept his progress a secret from his parents until, one day, we invited them to come at mealtime to see what he was capable of. They burst into tears of joy when they witnessed what they had never dreamed possible.

Our centre was part of a study that a psychology professor from the University of Manitoba was conducting. The study compared five different centres to determine what kind of a milieu was most successful in helping our clients learn these skills. The professor hired a research assistant named Bruce Tallman to gather data from the clients at each of the centres to determine the effectiveness of the various program settings. Because we were so accustomed to our all-female staff, we were very enthusiastic about greeting the new male researcher on the day of his first visit.

The moment Bruce appeared inside our doors, he was greeted by Jim, one of our higher-functioning clients. Each morning, Jim arrived with his hair neatly gelled in place, decked out in dress pants and a crisp, freshly ironed shirt. To complete his spiffy outfit, he always had a bowtie clipped to his collar. At first glance, he appeared to be one of the staff. Bruce stood near the entrance hesitantly, looking around for a place to set his briefcase and hang his coat. Before one of the staff had a chance to greet him, Jim walked up to Bruce, looked him right in the eye, and, in a condescending tone of voice, said, "Dummkopf!" (loosely translated as "stupid head"). I was quick to rescue Bruce from this overwhelming greeting, and when he realized that Jim wasn't one of the staff, he breathed a huge sigh of relief and we almost split our sides laughing about the bizarre incident.

The first thing I noticed about Bruce was his height. I always thought I was tall at five foot six, but my head was barely level with Bruce's chest. His slim build made his six-foot-three frame seem even more towering. *He is so tall!* was my first thought. I noticed everything about him. His blue eyes, his long, slender, neatly manicured fingers. His exotic flowered shirt and colour-coordinated pants, his shiny, stylish boots. He was so different from every other man I knew at that time. But most of all, it was his manner that caught my attention. He listened respectfully when I talked to him. He seemed interested in our clients and was gentle and kind with them. He surreptitiously took in everything about me, noting my long, dark hair, my vital energy, my high principles and values. He was instantly smitten; although, at the time, I was oblivious to his intentions. I found him interesting and fascinating, but felt no romantic inclinations after meeting him the first few times.

When he became more comfortable, Bruce started finding ways to attract my attention. He asked me to go out for lunch with him. I was quick to respond that I wasn't interested. I was dating a young man at the time, and even though we had no formal commitment to each other, I had no intention of going out with more than one guy at a time. Bruce was not easily deterred, and I guess it was his persistence that finally made me agree to go out for lunch with him. During that outing, I made it perfectly clear that I had no interest in dating him.

On days when he was gathering the data from our clients, Bruce joined the day care staff in the lunchroom. We got into some interesting debates. He was totally enthralled by the Mennonite community. He asked a lot of questions about our beliefs and practices. He was clearly quite spellbound by our faith, but made it clear that he did not share our belief in God.

"Can Mennonites marry non-Mennonites?" he asked innocently.

His question left me feeling both amused and astonished. I cannot remember what I said out loud, but my thoughts were: *Did he actually just say that?*

From that time, Bruce became increasingly clear about winning me over. One day, he approached me when I was in a back room teaching one of our clients how to wash her hands and face. I could sense that he wanted to talk to me, but I was absorbed in what I was doing. Self-consciously, he cleared his throat and stepped closer to me. "I have something for you," he said in a voice that was just above a whisper. He fished a folded piece of paper out of his back pocket and offered it to me. I dried my hands on a paper towel and reached out my hand. I slowly unfolded the paper and started reading the words on the page. In his own handwriting, he had written a poem for me. The poem was titled "Queen Anne's Lace."

It was brimming with romantic language whose raw beauty stirred something inside of me that was longing to be awakened. I was stunned. Nobody had ever written a poem for me before!

A wave of warmth spread slowly from my neck and into my cheeks. I knew I was blushing. I don't remember what I said to him, but I know I offered my gratitude and surprise. I also knew that it was futile to keep resisting the powerful force that was drawing me to this man, this man who wanted nothing more than to have me love him back.

My heart was literally being torn in two. I knew that my parents would vehemently oppose my going out with someone who did not share our beliefs. And it wasn't only my parents that I was worried about, it was the whole community. I feared rejection and ostracism. I would be seen as disloyal. I would be seen as turning my back on all the beliefs that I had been raised with, beliefs that I had internalized as my own.

I began a clandestine relationship with Bruce. I arranged for him to call me on the phone at the daycare centre at night, when nobody else was around. I could not risk having him call me at home. We would talk for hours. We wrote ten-page letters to each other, spilling our lives onto paper. I was definitely falling in love, hopelessly and against my better judgment. My parents and family were oblivious to the relationship that was developing between us, and for the time being, that was how I intended to keep it.

As our relationship progressed, I continued to feel utterly conflicted about my loyalties to the only family I had ever known and to a man with whom I had fallen in love. I was living a double life. It haunted me, and, for the first time in my life, frightening feelings of anxiety engulfed me. I was facing an unbearable impasse. Then, just as I was preparing to tell him that I could not continue our relationship, Bruce kissed me, gently and passionately. My heart melted. The tenderness and love he showed me was sweeter than anything I had ever felt before. The decision was made for me. I was ready to announce my love for him to the world. Whatever rejection I would face was going to be worth it. When I told my boyfriend that I was ending our relationship, it turned out that he was actually more serious about me than he had ever been willing to admit. Too bad for him—and good for Bruce.

Our courtship progressed quickly. Bruce asked me to marry him. There was no question; I said, "Yes!"

I could sense an attitude of disapproval around my decision to marry Bruce. Some of these sentiments were latent, but there was also overt opposition. The night before our wedding, I received a phone call from Greta, my former boss at the daycare centre where I met Bruce. "Grace, this marriage will never work," she told me bluntly. I was utterly stunned at her lack of support and understanding. There were other comments that were equally disheartening. My immediate family was outwardly supportive about our relationship, but their reluctance to give me their wholehearted blessing tore me apart for years.

Our Marriage

*A successful marriage requires falling in
love many times, always with the same person.*
—Mignon McLaughlin

Our wedding was a very simple affair. We were married in my parents' backyard by the minister from my childhood church. We had taken a huge risk with the weather, but an outdoor wedding was a dream that both of us valued. I guess it was a vestige of our leftover hippy mindset. The July day couldn't have been more perfect. A few cottony clouds scudded through the light-blue sky. The temperature was comfortably warm. The air was clear, with no hint of rain or humidity. My parents had had the exterior of the house freshly painted for the momentous occasion. The grass was mowed to perfection. Red geraniums, orange and yellow marigolds, pink sweet peas, and multi-coloured zinnias blossomed in clay pots and in the large flower garden in front of the house. We'd invited 200 guests to witness our vows to each other: "In sickness and in health, till death do us part." In addition to the traditional vows, we wrote our own. I included that I would accept Bruce just as he was and that I would not try to change him.

We began our married life in the cozy, quaint apartment where Bruce had been living by himself for the past year. The apartment occupied the entire third floor of a stately old house near downtown Winnipeg. The street was shaded by a canopy of graceful elm trees. We enjoyed many a picnic lunch on the lofty fire escape outside the bedroom window. It was so romantic to be up near the treetops with the squirrels and singing birds. We could reach out our hands and touch the sky. Through the leafy foliage, we could see a century-old stone church, which sat on the corner directly across from our apartment. Our line of vision was level with its tall bell tower, which kept track of passing time with hourly chimes.

Before we were married, my mom and aunts hosted a bridal shower for me. One of the games at the shower included an activity in which everyone wrote a piece of marital advice for me on an index card. I clearly remember once piece of advice from a staid old aunt: "Don't spoil your husband." I found this quite amusing, but it didn't take long for me to renege on this bit of wisdom. Soon after our marriage, I subconsciously began following the patterns I had witnessed in my mother. The wife cooks all the meals and defers to her husband in all matters.

They say that a woman marries someone just like their dad. How wrong they were this time. There was no imaginable likeness between Bruce and my dad. Bruce's DNA did not contain one strand of "farmer." He was a city boy, through and through. I was fascinated by the huge contrast in his background, upbringing, and personality. Bruce was as methodical and logical as my dad was impulsive and spontaneous. Over the years, I would learn that I needed a lot of patience to get used to Bruce's way of doing things. I had become accustomed to quick, decisive action from my dad. A good example of this contrast occurred when a tree was to be cut down at the Tallman cottage. It took several days of back-and-forth discussion to decide how to go about this task. The actual job of cutting the tree down took the better part of another day. I knew that my dad would have completed the job in fewer than ten minutes.

Bruce and I had grown up with very different expectations around household chores. In my family, everyone was expected to do their part. Cooking, cleaning, dishwashing, and other duties were responsibilities that we bore as soon as we were capable. I recall rinsing dishes while standing on a chair before I was tall enough to reach the kitchen sink. Playing was seen as a privilege that you earned after all the chores were done. Bruce, on the other hand, was waited on by his mother throughout his life. She did not expect her children to help out and made very few demands of them. It is not surprising that the issue of housework became a bone of contention in our marriage.

Somehow, I expected Bruce to read my mind and offer to help around the house and take more responsibility with raising the children. By example, my mother had taught me that asking for what you need is not an option. It would be many years before I would learn to become more assertive and state my needs clearly. I would come to recognize the obvious truth that nobody could read my mind. Unfortunately, while our children were growing up, I had not reached this point, and I often struggled with bottled-up resentment. These unspoken feelings took a huge toll on my emotional well-being.

Three years into our marriage, our daughter Hailey was born. I eagerly anticipated her birth. I worked as a pediatric nurse at that time and I thought I was as prepared as anyone could be to take on the maternal role. I knew all about childhood illnesses, immunizations, and optimal approaches to parenting. But I quickly discovered that actually having a little baby to care for twenty-four hours a day was very different from having professional knowledge about parenting.

Hailey, our firstborn, was beautiful and healthy. However, she suffered from colic and cried lustily for long periods of time. She did not have a regular sleep pattern, and I quickly discovered that being a parent meant enduring lack of sleep, night after night, no matter how exhausted I was. Because I was attempting to breastfeed her, Bruce basically left her care to me. He felt helpless with her crying and assumed that I was the only one who could offer her comfort and provide for her basic needs.

Bruce was in the middle of writing and rewriting his master's thesis in religious studies. He was not used to having a crying baby in the house and begged me to keep her quiet so that he could concentrate on his academic pursuits. I took Hailey on long walks in her carriage. She seemed to settle with the rocking motion and sometimes fell asleep while we were walking. Unfortunately, while she napped, I was under a great deal of pressure to type and retype Bruce's many revisions. That was back in the days before computers, and with each of the many changes, I had to start from the beginning and retype the entire manuscript. I did not get an opportunity to rest during the day. I found myself becoming more and more worn out to the point where I lost all interest in eating and could not fall asleep at night.

In desperation, I bundled Hailey up with all her baby paraphernalia and drove to my parents' farm. Maybe Bruce would finally be able to complete his thesis if he had some peace and quiet. I felt ignored and frustrated. His mind was completely absorbed with his writing. My mother took one look at me and immediately sensed my depleted physical and emotional resources. In her motherly way, she reached out to help in the best way she could. She offered to look after Hailey at night so that I could get some much-needed rest. Unfortunately, I was too wound up and tense to get any sleep, despite the respite my mother provided. With my acute lack of sleep, depression was starting to settle in. My mood plummeted and I knew I needed help. I could not go on much longer in this state. By this time, I had given up on breastfeeding. My milk supply was completely depleted. I made an appointment to see my obstetrician. He was accustomed to dealing with new mothers in this predicament and prescribed some medication to help me sleep.

When Hailey and I returned to our home in Winnipeg, Bruce announced that he had been offered a once-in-a-lifetime opportunity to travel to India with a group of other students. The trip would last for six weeks and all of his expenses would be paid for through a scholarship. I tried very hard to share his enthusiasm, but all I could think of was that I would be left alone to adjust to my new role as a parent. I was already feeling abandoned by the endless hours he spent on his thesis. As so often was the case, I was being asked to sacrifice my own needs and best interests to a greater cause. In the end, I realized that neither of us could live with the disappointment if Bruce did not take advantage of this rare chance.

For the next six weeks, I continued to struggle with dark feelings of depression. I relied on my mother for overnight respite and maternal encouragement. Hailey gradually outgrew her colic and slept for longer periods. The thrill of seeing her reach all the expected milestones of infant development became a source of joy that gradually lifted my mood.

After several more years of non-stop effort, Bruce finally completed his master's degree at the University of Toronto. It was here that our son, Brandon, was born. Hailey was three years old and helped us welcome her baby brother into our little family with great excitement. We loved our adorable little boy, and luckily, I had a much easier time after his birth and did not experience the same depression that I'd had when Hailey was born.

Toronto was a vibrant and exciting city, and we had hoped to stay there after Bruce finished his studies. Unfortunately, it was also exorbitantly expensive. Bruce was out of work, and I was looking after two small children. We were in a desperate financial situation. We dreamed of buying our own home, and we knew we could not afford to settle in Toronto. After much debate and discussion, we reluctantly realized that Winnipeg was a much more affordable city and moved back there. There, our dream of home ownership came true. We bought a cozy little bungalow near the University of Manitoba. My mother's health was rapidly declining, and I was grateful to be near her. Now that I was strong and emotionally thriving, I could turn the tables and offer her support when she was in need of it.

Bruce, our children, and I started putting our roots down, thinking this was to be our home for years to come. I recall many happy family times in those early years. Bruce was very creative in thinking up little games to play with Hailey and Brandon. Two of them were "placker" and "spooing." I don't advise you to google these words, as they won't have any linguistic significance to someone not directly involved. The placker game was a combination of hide-and-seek and tag. Bruce would hide behind the couch, and as the children ran past him, he would lunge out of hiding and they'd have to run as fast as they could to avoid being tackled by their dad. I have no idea how they were able to wind down and fall asleep after their wild shrieking and laughter, but it was a nightly ritual that they could not miss. The spooing game was simply giving loud "raspberry" kisses on their bare bellies. "Do it again," they would beg, never tiring of the silliness and fun.

Bruce continued to struggle with finding full-time work, and we relied on my income as a part-time emergency nurse to supplement our livelihood.

When Bruce was offered a permanent, full-time job in London, Ontario, I was eager and excited. For me, it was a no-brainer. What an opportunity! Bruce, in his usual fashion, agonized over the decision. By nature, he was much more cautious than I was. He carefully considered all the possible angles and took his time before accepting the position.

Once he did, we packed all our earthly belongings into a moving van and made the long trek back east to Ontario. It was late July when we arrived, and we were not prepared for the suffocating humidity and oppressive heat that greeted us. Temperatures were in the high thirties as we settled into our new house in South London. With no air conditioning, it felt like we were living in a sauna. That first night, we experienced the most ferocious thunderstorm we had ever encountered. Git Git, our orange tabby cat, who had endured the long journey from Winnipeg with us, had cautiously ventured out earlier in the evening. "Where's Git Git?" Brandon asked, his face scrunched up in a worried expression as thunder and lightning exploded around us. I opened the screen door a crack and called his name. My voice was drowned out by the wild gusts of wind and the pounding rain. I was just about to close the door when Git Git shot inside as if propelled by a rocket. We all burst out laughing. For the moment, our tension had been broken, but the storm continued for another few hours into the darkness of the night.

Living in a new city was an exciting challenge, and life soon took on a comfortable rhythm. Bruce and I both settled into the routine of working. Bruce, in his new job as the director of a Catholic adult education centre, was eager to begin a full-time role that was relevant to his educational qualifications. I was hired as a part-time RN in the coronary-care unit of a London hospital. In September, Hailey and Brandon began attending their new school, which was within comfortable walking distance from our house. Hailey had no trouble plunging into new friendships. Brandon did not adjust quite as easily. He missed his friends in Winnipeg terribly, but gradually, he, too, made new friends.

Things seemed to be humming along smoothly. London had become our new home, a new beginning. Life, for the most part, was good, but I couldn't shake the feelings of loss after my mother's death.

She died a few months before our move to London. I remembered her incredible suffering and the toll it had taken on our family, especially on my dad. I couldn't help feeling a little bit guilty for abandoning him at a time when he was feeling lost and alone without Mom at his side. I consoled myself with the thought that he still had several of his children living nearby to offer their comfort and practical help.

My experience with my mother's illness and death kindled a deep desire in me to help others who were going through similarly difficult situations. I started taking courses at King's College in London in the thanatology department. Thanatology is the study of death and dying, which might seem a little morbid to the average person. However, my recent experience had left me curious and open to everything that was related to this topic. I enrolled in the grief and bereavement certificate program with the intention to learn as much as I could. I had a goal to use my knowledge to reach out to others who were dealing with grief and loss. I took it a step further and signed up for training to become a hospital chaplain.

Hospital Chaplaincy Training

The purpose of learning is growth, and our minds, unlike our bodies, can continue growing as we continue to live.
—Mortimer Adler

I was granted a leave of absence from my nursing job. For the next three months I attended a full-time training program for hospital chaplains. I assumed we would be given concise, how-to instructions, complete with a manual on how to go about working as a chaplain. I was unprepared for the intense process of self-reflection into which we were launched.

As chaplains, we would encounter life-and-death situations, as well as more routine day-to-day encounters with people who were struggling with illness, pain, and questions of faith, values, and meaning. We would be dealing with people of all religious beliefs and cultural backgrounds. It was imperative that we be cognizant of our life journey, thus far, in order to be aware of how we responded to various situations in our own lives. It was as if a huge mirror was being held up to my life so that I could come face-to-face with my own beliefs and experiences.

One of our initial assignments was to relate our life history. My classmate Anna and I interviewed one another for this. Our task was to uncover how we dealt with issues within our family of origin, our strengths and weaknesses, how we responded to stress and pressure, and anything else that made us who we were. No stone was left unturned as our lives were held up, as if to a spotlight. After writing an in-depth account of each other's lives, we presented our partner's stories to the rest of our classmates and supervisors. It was almost as if we were surgically dissecting all aspects of our lives and exposing ourselves to people who, at this point, were almost complete strangers.

It was my first exposure to this kind of deep, personal examination, and initially, I found it to be very uncomfortable. I discovered things about myself that I had taken completely for granted. For the first time, I recognized that I had been raised with completely black-and-white religious beliefs and values that left no room for an alternative viewpoint. I also acknowledged, for the first time, the impact of my father's harsh punishment on my well-being and self-esteem. I felt like the rug had been pulled out from under me. I had always felt very secure with my beliefs and upbringing and had never thought to question them or expose them to scrutiny. Suddenly, I was being asked to do just that.

We were informed that self-awareness was our greatest tool as chaplains. Without this skill, we were doomed to repeat patterns and behaviours that did not serve us well. We needed to be confident that, when dealing with a patient's issues, our own personal reactions would not get in the way. We needed to know what situations triggered our own issues and to be vigilant at all times that our focus remain on the patient, not on ourselves. We were instructed in the essentials of self-care and setting boundaries in our lives. We were taught how to become assertive with our needs and desires, a skill I was sadly lacking. I had always prided myself in having a strong ability to empathize with others, a character trait that, without personal boundaries and assertiveness, had left me open to people taking advantage of me. I had learned well from my mother. My eyes were opened to the fact that when I ignored my own needs, I left myself open to resentment. The crisp, clear communication of my needs was a skill I lacked, and developing this new way of relating to others was going to be a lengthy and challenging process. All of this training was like embarking on a new frontier. Once I overcame the initial shock to this new approach to life, I became excited and recognized that I had just been awarded a gift that would help me function in a much healthier way than ever before. My chaplaincy training became like a watershed experience.

My initial reluctant reaction to the training soon gave way to awe and amazement. I was astounded at how much I was growing and maturing in my own personal development as a result of the new self-understanding I was gaining. I knew that I wanted to take another session of the training and eventually work as a chaplain.

It turned out that, within a few years, I would be hired to work as a chaplain at a large rehabilitation and veteran's hospital in London. It was the beginning of another fulfilling and meaningful chapter of my life.

Positive Pregnancy Test

It is not the strongest of the species that survive, nor the most intelligent, but the ones most responsive to change.
—Charles Darwin

Our little family was sitting down at the kitchen table when the phone rang. Our daughter, Hailey, by now a teenager, and our son, Brandon, who was eleven, were sitting across from each other. Bruce sat at the end opposite to me. We were getting ready to dig into a big bowl of steaming spaghetti with a homemade meat sauce. My chair was nearest the phone, so I was the one who answered. *Probably a telemarketer*, I thought to myself. They always call at supper time. With that in mind, I answered rather brusquely. The voice at the other end was familiar, but it took me several seconds to identify her.

"Hello, Grace?" It was Dr. Graham, my family doctor. I went to see her last week because I had been feeling a little off—no energy, mild nausea, with a bloated stomach. "Your pregnancy test came back. It's positive." Stunned silence.

"Grace, are you there?"

How can this be? I thought to myself. We have always been careful to use protection. "Oh, no," I managed to gasp. Again, silence.

"I think we had better arrange an appointment so we can talk about this," she said. Her tone was empathetic.

My response was obviously not what she had been expecting to hear. The call was over, but I stood holding the receiver in my hand with a dazed expression on my face. I had entertained the remotest suspicion that this might be what was wrong with me, but to hear it in plain English, at such an unexpected time, threw me off balance completely. My facial expression betrayed the fact that I had received unwelcome news, but I was not prepared to say it out loud. I brushed the questions from Hailey and Bruce aside. This was not the time to talk about it. I don't remember if I ate any supper that night; my thoughts were elsewhere.

When the dishes were cleared away and Hailey and Brandon were doing their homework, I flung my arms around Bruce and started sobbing. Hot tears soaked the shoulder of his sweater. I blurted the news to him. I don't think he quite understood why this devastated me so deeply. We had discussed the remote possibility that I might be pregnant, but both of us had brushed it aside as being very unlikely. Now it was reality. I was forty-one years old, my youngest child was eleven years old, and I had just started a new career as a hospital chaplain. But my most vivid fear was a recurrence of postpartum depression. After Hailey's birth, I had suffered from a deep depression for four months. I knew the statistics: the strongest determinant of postpartum depression is having had it before.

My appointment with Dr. Graham took place the following week. I cried for the first fifteen minutes of our session. She couldn't have been more understanding. She expended a great deal of effort to see things from my perspective. Because I was in my early forties, she offered me an amniocentesis, which would determine if there were any anomalies in the fetus. I knew that abortion wasn't an option for me, so what was the point? Dr. Graham told me, in a matter-of-fact tone, that if I planned to continue the pregnancy, I needed to move ahead with a positive attitude and make the best of my situation. I took her advice to heart, in the best way I could. Somehow, everything would work out in the end.

That evening, we told the kids that we had a special surprise for them. We took them out to Pizza Hut and, over pepperoni-and-mushroom pizza, told them the news that they would be getting a little brother or sister in about seven months. Both Hailey and Brandon burst into tears, but each for a different reason. Hailey's tears were happy ones. She said she had always wanted to have a baby sister, and she was overjoyed. Brandon wasn't so sure he wanted to be nudged out of his special rank of baby of the family.

When we got home, Hailey went straight to her room and wrote a beautiful letter to her unknown baby sister or brother (she was hoping for a sister). Brandon resumed the video game he had been playing, and having a more introspective personality, kept his thoughts to himself.

With long, curly, blonde hair and eyes the colour of jade, Hailey was a striking beauty. She was in the eighth grade at a special school for music and art. She had the opportunity to learn to play the viola in her school orchestra and sang beautiful, angelic music in the choir. She was a budding artist. The year before, she had entered an art contest sponsored by a veterans' association. The contest had involved creating a poster for Remembrance Day. She drew a cross that was decked with poppies. Underneath the picture were the haunting words: "What have we done?" Her entry was selected as the first-prize winner. She was awarded a dozen Disney videos as her reward. These movies provided endless hours of entertainment for the whole family.

Hailey had the gift of being outspoken and honest. It was never difficult to guess what was going on in her mind, because she expressed her feelings and thoughts unreservedly. Perhaps she had been given the role of being our family spokesperson, because the rest of us were rather quiet and introverted. Hailey surrounded herself with friends from school and our neighbourhood. She loved popular music and was madly in love with Joey Joe from New Kids on the Block. Her bedroom walls and ceiling were plastered with posters of this musical group.

From a very young age, she demonstrated a keen, inquiring mind. When I was pregnant with Brandon and she was three years old, she asked some very inquisitive questions. "Is there a crib in your stomach?" She was very concerned about where the baby slept while in my womb. She also asked me,

"Is it dark inside your stomach, Mommy?" I didn't know how to respond, but she quickly answered her own question by saying, "It's OK; there's a light at the end of the hall."

Brandon, our handsome dude, was three years younger than Hailey. He was gifted in many ways of his own. He had an athletic build and could wallop a mighty Taekwondo kick. He was obsessed with football. He was an avid fan of the San Francisco 49ers and adored Joe Montana. He later played the position of quarterback on the local community football team, much to his parents' pride and joy.

His loyalty and devotion to his small circle of friends were admirable. He valued his friendships and enjoyed nothing more than roughhousing with them in our backyard or shooting hoops in our driveway. A favourite family activity involved hiking in the woods with Brandon and one of his friends. One Sunday afternoon, we found ourselves wandering languidly amid the red and gold autumn trees, completely absorbed in the beauty of the forest around us. At one point, we realized that we were wandering in circles; we had passed a spreading oak tree several times, and we could not find our way out of the forest. The sky clouded over and a cool drizzle began falling, leaving us damp and shivering. We eventually found the path that took us back to our car. Had it not been for Brandon's keen observations of the landmarks, we might still be drifting around in a lost state.

When Brandon was about three years old, he went through a phase where he was obsessed with dinosaurs. He knew the names of every dinosaur imaginable and could pronounce the challenging names of each one of them. Names like pterodactyl rolled off his tongue effortlessly. His all-time favourite was triceratops.

Once Hailey began attending school, Brandon and I shared a lot of quality time together. He accompanied me on my errands, whether it was grocery shopping or going to the mall. One day, we passed a shop window, and Brandon excitedly pointed to a purse in the window, "Hailey would like that," he said. He was always cognizant of others' needs and wishes. One day, we went out for lunch at a restaurant. A lady, who was a complete stranger, approached us and commented on how well-behaved Brandon was. That's my boy!

At Home with My New Baby

*Courage is resistance to, and mastery of fear,
not the absence of fear.*
—Jane McGonigal

Hailey and Brandon could hardly wait for me and Alana to come home from the hospital. The day had finally arrived when they could greet their new baby sister. "Can I hold her?" Hailey begged. With some instruction in supporting her little head, and after making sure she was seated securely on the living room sofa, I placed Alana in Hailey's lap. She was bursting with affection and self-importance as she cradled her tiny sister. Brandon showered Alana with loving kisses. After watching Hailey for a few minutes, he had his turn at holding her.

After the initial excitement wore off, our family settled back into the usual routines. I survived by switching into automatic pilot. My mood was still in a very dark place, but somehow I managed to resume my role of dutiful mother and wife.

Brandon's teacher, Mrs. Matthews, had followed my pregnancy with great interest. She seemed almost as excited about Alana's birth as Brandon. She invited me and Alana to come to Brandon's classroom where, together with all his classmates, they threw an amazing baby shower for us. I think she was secretly using our experience as a teaching tool about family life. We were a living demonstration of what it was like to welcome a new baby into a home for her students. Brandon's classmates adored Alana, and Brandon practically exploded with pride as he held his baby sister in front of his friends. I did my best to find joy in this beautiful moment. For a brief moment, I forgot about my depression and soaked up the positive energy of the experience.

Meanwhile, Bruce had changed employment. He was now working in a job similar to the one he had worked at in London, except it was in Sarnia, an hour's drive away. Rather than commuting each day, he stayed overnight twice a week. I missed his presence and support. Bruce seemed to begrudge the time I devoted to caring for Alana. I think he felt abandoned and confused with the changes in routine. He was stressed with the commuting and the pressures of a full-time job. After his long commute, he wanted nothing more than to sit down to a homemade meal when he got home at night. He seemed to have no understanding of the physical drain involved in breastfeeding a newborn baby. I struggled to keep up with feeding Alana as often as she needed. I had read all the literature on breastfeeding, and as a nurse, I knew that it was considered to be the gold standard of infant nutrition. The antibodies passed on through breast milk were essential for the baby's health and well-being.

My exhausted body was wracked with tension. Sleep evaded me. I constantly felt on edge, as if there was an unseen threat of physical danger just around the corner. I felt like I was on the brink of falling over a precipice into a dark, bottomless abyss. My fight-or-flight instincts were perpetually on red alert. Alana continued to nurse like a pro, latching on with a strong sucking reflex, but my milk supply was rapidly drying up. Giving up on breastfeeding was a huge disappointment, but it was becoming clear that there was no alternative. I experienced feelings of guilt and inadequacy as a mother.

Bruce and I had been planning a family holiday to drive to Manitoba over the previous few months. Hailey and Brandon were registered to attend a summer camp that was operated by my family's church. It would be a time for them to connect with their cousins and have fun swimming, canoeing, and just enjoying a carefree getaway on a beautiful lake near the Ontario–Manitoba border.

Part of the plan involved staying with Bruce's family at their cottage for a week. The cottage conjured up images of stinging mosquitoes, cramped, rustic quarters, with outdoor washrooms. There would be no privacy, no way to keep a crying baby from waking up the entire household. I shuddered at the thought. I wasn't coping at home; how could I manage a three-week trip with a newborn baby?

That night, my sleeplessness didn't coincide with Alana's feeding schedule. I lay awake through the long, dark night, wondering how I could possibly go on this family trip. I didn't want to spoil the plans that everyone had been looking forward to for months. Bruce and the kids needed a holiday, a break from the daily grind.

When morning arrived, I had made up my mind. I would stay home with Alana. The rest of the family would have to go on their planned adventure without me. Coming to a decision was a huge relief. The mountain of uncertainty and anxiety about driving to Manitoba had been scaled. It was an uphill struggle, robbing me of much-needed sleep, but I had arrived on the other side. It was the right choice, the only option I was capable of at the time. Maybe it would be a break for me as well, with only myself and Alana to look after. I could sleep when she slept and there would be no pressure to cook meals for anyone. It might even feel like a holiday for me. I would catch up on my sleep and rest whenever Alana slept. No pressure to do anything else.

The morning of departure arrived. All the suitcases and sleeping bags were trundled into the trunk. I handed them the lunch I had packed: peanut butter-and-jam sandwiches, apples, a bag of their favourite gummy bears, juice, and a package of store-bought cookies. Bruce enveloped me in his strong arms and kissed me and Alana goodbye. "You're sure you don't want to come with us?" he asked pleadingly. I shook my head. No, I was making the only decision that made sense for me and Alana. I felt a sense of relief. I was using my assertiveness skills that I had learned as a chaplain, and setting boundaries to protect what I deemed to be in my best interests. To be honest, I really had no alternative; I wasn't well enough to travel 2,000 miles with a baby.

Grace Tallman

Bruce backed the car out of the driveway; his mind was already focused on the long drive ahead of them. Hailey and Brandon hung out the car windows, waving and blowing us kisses. I waved back as I stood outside the front door, hugging Alana. I tried to convince myself that we would be all right, that by the time they returned, I would be back to my usual strong, healthy self. I had no idea how wrong I was.

Rock Bottom

*Success is not measured by how high someone climbs, but by
how high they bounce when they hit bottom.*
—George S. Patton

Unfortunately, my depression did not go on a holiday. Alana was sleeping more often, but her timing was completely unpredictable. Sometimes her naps lasted two hours; sometimes, she would awaken after only ten or fifteen minutes. Even though she was sleeping for longer periods at night, I found myself tossing and turning and lying awake for hours. I craved sleep. Every inch of me longed for deep, oblivious, mindless, restorative nothingness. When I finally managed to fall into a restless sleep, I was tormented with a recurring nightmare.

I am a deer caught in the headlights of an oncoming car. Desperately, I try to avoid the rushing of the vehicle that is coming at me, but the lights blind me. I try to jump aside but the car sideswipes me, leaving me bruised and bleeding at the side of the road—not quite dead, but gasping for air, bleeding profusely, too weak to get up. I am that injured deer, needing to take care of my newborn fawn, waiting for someone to notice my wounded, helpless state, someone to stay by my side until I am ready to get up on my wobbly legs. Surely someone will notice my desperation, my vulnerable state. I am too weak to call for help; I need someone to stop at the side of the road and gently lift me on their shoulders and carry me to a safe place, tend to my wounds, and tell me it will be all right.

My mind was taken over by a monster that just wouldn't relent. I was filled with overwhelming thoughts of hopelessness and despair. There was no tomorrow and no yesterday, only a tenacious NOW that threatened to suffocate me. The dark cloud hovered menacingly on my horizon, filtering out positive emotions, robbing me of sleep. A monochromatic blanket shrouded my mind—sometimes dark blackness, sometimes grey, and sometimes no colour at all.

My thoughts became increasingly irrational and far-flung. They were coming from a place far away, from a coal-black, unrecognizable place. I did not initiate these hopeless thoughts; some hideous intruder had invaded my mind and was playing a cruel game with me. Perhaps some of this menacing introspection emanated from the dark secret corner in my brain that I had walled off since fifth grade. The intruder was strong and intimidating, filling my head with things I would never dream of on my own. This was not a feeling of sadness that could be explained by some kind of tragedy or loss. This was a deep despondency in the face of what should have been cause for joy and celebration. My thoughts turned ominously to death. I did not want to go on fighting this battle. I was losing my grip on life. I was tiring of the struggle to keep my head above water. I became increasingly obsessed with killing myself. I ruminated about ways to do it. I knew if I died, there would be no one to take care of Alana. The only way out was for both of us to go together. I visualized taking poison, and putting some in Alana's bottle. We would die together. We would escape this dark world and be free of the torment of this dark depression. My contact with reality was diminished to a few fragile strands. I functioned mechanically. Ironically, I continued to lovingly care for Alana. I prepared formula, fed her regularly, changed her diapers, bathed her, held her close, and watched over her. It was my boundless love for her that kept me from following through with the horrifying impulses that were hounding me.

The only logical response I could think of to ease my inner turmoil was to keep my body in perpetual motion. Day after day, pushing Alana's stroller, I walked for hours at a time. I have no idea how many miles we covered. I completely lost track of time and distance. Somehow, the mindless act of putting one foot in front of the other, over and over again, had a soothing effect on my mental state. As I became more and more obsessed with walking, the pounds melted off my body. I paid little attention to eating, and my clothes hung on my dwindling frame like a loose tent. Apart from the obvious weight loss and restless activity, nobody looking in on my life would have noticed the blackness that was devouring me from the inside. They would have thought: How lovely. A happy young mother on a walk with her little baby.

In the face of my overwhelming depression, I longed for the comfort of my mother's unconditional love and support. I missed her desperately and mourned the fact that she would never meet her newest grandchild. I could think of no one else who could even begin to understand what I was going through. There was no one to talk to; I was completely alone. The freedom and relief I had envisioned staying home alone with Alana had turned into feelings of abandonment. I felt deserted. How could Bruce leave us when he knew how fragile I was? I resented his absence. He had no idea what I was going through, and I wasn't even sure he was interested in knowing.

A faint voice began reasoning with me, whispering through the darkness. "Dr. Graham would understand," it said. The voice persisted until I recognized its wisdom.

"Of course," I said to myself. "Why didn't I think of that before?" It didn't take long for Dr. Graham to see the emotional pain I was suffering. She prescribed a low dose of Prozac. I had been very hesitant to take medications in the past, but it did not take any convincing for me to try this avenue if there was even a remote possibility that it would bring relief.

"I want to see you next week to see how you are doing," she said. She warned that it could take up to four weeks for me to experience any positive effects. For the first time since Alana's birth, I felt a faint glimmer of hope.

Bruce and the two older children were due to return from their vacation in just over a week. They would never know just how close I had come to the edge while they were gone.

The Birds Still Sing

By the time they got home, I was starting to feel my mood lifting ever so slightly. With each passing day, I gradually felt the depression fading.

Return to Darkness

*If you ever think of giving up, remember
why you held on for so long.*
—Hayley Williams

My maternity leave was quickly coming to an end. I could not believe how time had elapsed. We settled Alana in with a babysitter who lived just down the street. I returned to work. I loved my work as a chaplain. It's what I was good at. By now, my depression was nothing more than a bad memory. The Prozac that Dr. Graham prescribed was doing its job. I had finally reached the other side of sadness. My happiness was in stark contrast to the debilitating depression I had experienced a few months earlier. In my newfound state of well-being, I could barely even remember that I ever felt depressed. My energy and zest for life had returned. I was feeling on top of my game. I felt confident; life was full of meaning again. I lapped up the "welcome back" colleagues who had missed my presence while I was on maternity leave, extended to me.

I was a chaplain bringing comfort to patients who were struggling with devastating challenges. There were people with spinal cord injuries resulting in paraplegia, wondering if they would ever walk again. Some patients had suffered traumatic brain injuries, their personalities shattered and unrecognizable to their families. Patients were looking for answers, begging me to infuse hope into their exploded lives. I listened deeply to World War II veterans whose lives had been shattered by the ravages of war more than fifty years earlier. They had endured the explosions of bombs and shrapnel wounds. They had witnessed brothers and combat partners blasted to shreds in front of their eyes. They continued to live the horrors of war every day of their lives. None of them would ever be the same again. But I was there to pick up the pieces for them. I was in the role that I loved. I thrived on being there for others in their life challenges.

I threw myself into my work with passion. I was so relieved to feel normal again that I ignored the flashing orange caution lights that were trying to tell me to slow down. The reality of juggling my full-time work as a chaplain, caring for a six-month-old baby, being a loving mother to an eleven-year-old and an energetic and rebellious fourteen-year-old came crashing down on me. The pressure only got worse. Things between Bruce and me were ragged. I desperately craved his love and understanding. He didn't seem to understand how much I needed his support. He was burdened with his work pressures and the commuting. He often came home from work exhausted and irritable. He wondered why I was not pulling my weight when dinner was not ready and waiting for him when he arrived. I was utterly stunned. He had no conception of how stretched I was with all my responsibilities. Rather than leaning on each other, we built a wall that seemed to get more impenetrable each day. Bruce's lack of support left me seething with feelings of resentment and bewilderment. Again, I felt deserted and alone.

I knew I was starting on a downward spiral, the depression once again taking hold. I recognized the unwelcome intruder that had had me in its clutches just a few months earlier, that tenacious, unrelenting grip of darkness. At first, going back to work had been a positive distraction, but it had quickly become an overwhelming stressor.

I dug deeper inside myself to find the strength and wisdom to come up with inspiring words to help my patients rebuild their shattered lives. I was supposed to be their spiritual cheerleader, but my enthusiasm and energy were rapidly fading. I felt only emptiness. My rich inner resources were rapidly becoming depleted.

I did not heed the warning signs that were begging me to slow my frantic pace. I pushed on, doggedly. It's unclear what the exact trigger was that caused my life to cave in around me, but I was in the middle of a workday and the next thing I knew, tears were streaming down my face. I was falling apart and there was nothing I could do to stop myself. I felt embarrassed and ashamed and raced to the privacy of my office where I put my head on my varnished oak desk. An ocean of tears burst a dam behind my eyelids, and no amount of effort could stem the flow. I was drowning. I needed a lifeline.

Any hope of the future was ripped away. I could see only the unbearable, agonizing present. There was no hope for me. The emotional pain was excruciating. I could not go on like this. The darkness had returned: black, suffocating, strangling. I was bound in a straitjacket of emotional pain. My only reality was searing, unrelenting blackness. There was no sun, no moon, no stars. I didn't want to go on. I couldn't go on.

Time became meaningless. I had no idea how much time passed. The only name that came to mind was Dr. Graham. I knew she cared. She would know what to do. Her office was within walking distance from the hospital where I worked. Mindlessly, I began walking there. The wind was biting and the sidewalk was covered in snow. Cars whizzed by on the busy street. I didn't notice any of this. The only thing I knew was that, somehow, I had to get to Dr. Graham's office. She had been my strength through the past few years. She had been there for me throughout my pregnancy. She knew the struggles I had experienced since giving birth. She was my only hope.

I sat on a red plastic upholstered chair. I didn't have an appointment, but I was desperate. "Dr. Graham will see you between patients," the receptionist informed me. I noticed her look of concern. My tears had not stopped flowing. She ushered me into an examining room to give me some privacy. People were staring.

Dr. Graham stepped into the room where I was waiting. She handed me a box of tissues. Her eyes conveyed concern and compassion. Between sobs, I told her, "I can't go on. I want to die." She understood. I didn't need to say anymore.

"I can't stay right now; I have another patient. Why don't you just wait here. I will be back as soon as I can."

And so our conversation continued, hour after hour, a little bit at a time. She was able to piece my story together. I must have gathered my wits about me sufficiently to call Hailey and ask her to pick Alana up from the babysitter. Everyone would be home by now. They must be wondering where I was. Dr. Graham picked up the phone and spoke to Bruce. "Grace needs to go to the hospital. Can you come to my office and pick her up?"

Getting Help

And the best part about rock bottom is
that you can only go up from there.
—Quinn Loftis

The details of my life were hazy for the next few hours. All I know is that, somehow, I got to the hospital where Dr. Graham had arranged for me to be assessed by a psychiatrist. I don't know how long I waited to be seen. It could have been hours; I simply don't remember. I was given a hospital gown and a robe. I was assigned to a room. I remember it having two beds that were separated by a pink polyester curtain suspended from a curving metal track in the ceiling. Like clothes in a washing machine, my mind became a jumble of disconnected thoughts. The room was spinning around me. Nothing felt real. The next thing I remember was observing myself, as if from a great distance. I saw myself standing on top of my bed. The belt from my robe was noosed around my neck. I was reaching up to the ceiling, trying to tie the other end of the belt onto the metal curtain track. At that moment, the psychiatrist walked in.

"What are you doing?" he shouted. I don't recall much else about the interaction. I don't remember the psychiatrist's name, or what he looked like. I know he said the words, "Form 1" in an accusing voice. He sounded angry and annoyed, like I was interfering with the plans for his evening.

The next memory I have is being loaded onto an ambulance stretcher. I have vague memories of talking to the admitting clerk at the regional mental health centre. I told her my address, my phone number, the name of my doctor, my emergency contact information. I remember signing on the bottom line. I distinctly recall the realization that I was now a patient. I was no longer a nurse or a chaplain. I was hospital property. I would be subject to their rules, their routines, their policies.

I was perfectly capable of walking, but the ambulance attendants insisted on wheeling my stretcher to the admitting ward. I stared up at the stained ceiling tiles and marked the distance of the long hallway by the regularly spaced fluorescent light bulbs that glared harshly down at me. I distinctly recall the rasping sound of the doorbell at the entrance of the ward where I was being admitted. We had to wait to be buzzed in by the nurses. I would be locked in. No escape.

I was unprepared for the feeling of relief that rushed over me. The locked unit and the constant presence of nurses gave me a feeling of security. For the moment, I would be safe, protected from the irrational impulses that raged inside me. I would get the help I needed for this dark depression. The tables had completely reversed. It was the very first time in my life when I was not the caregiver but the one being cared for.

I was ushered into a single room with a narrow bed.

I sat on the edge of my bed and went through the admission procedure. Molly was my admitting nurse. She was close to my age. Her reddish hair was stylishly bobbed. Molly checked my purse for contraband: medications, sharps, or anything that could be potentially used to harm myself or others. This felt intrusive, but rules are rules, and I reluctantly understood their intention. She handed me a bathrobe, which was conspicuously missing its belt. Molly seemed to genuinely care as she took my mental health and physical history. She nodded knowingly when I told her about my episodes of depression since giving birth. I told her about my brother Henry's suicide less than a year earlier. She seemed very interested in hearing more details about what happened with Henry. She thought this had a significant bearing on my own mental health. My eyelids blinked rapidly as the realization hit me. Of course, the suicide of a close family member would be a huge trigger for depression. Why had I not seen that very obvious connection earlier? My thoughts reverted back to that fateful New Year's Eve—the day when I was at work and was interrupted by the phone call from my dad.

My Brother Henry

*A person whose head is bowed and whose
eyes are heavy cannot look at the light.*
—Christine de Pizan

For some reason, as soon as I heard my dad's voice on the phone, I thought to myself: *Something has happened to Henry*. A long-distance call during my work day was entirely out of the ordinary. I will never know why I immediately assumed he was calling about Henry. Somehow, I just knew. My dad's next words left me frozen in shock: "Henry died last night." My mind started to protest. *He's only forty-three years old. This must be a terrible mistake!* The next thing I remember was making calls to the airlines to get a ticket to fly to Winnipeg. I had to get there as fast as I could to be with my family.

Growing up with eight brothers was quite an adventure! Henry was only two years older than me, so we had a lot in common. Henry dropped out of school for a year after completing grade ten. That meant we were in grade eleven at the same time. Sitting on the bed in his upstairs bedroom, we would quiz each other on algebra equations and remote history trivia in preparation for final exams.

Henry had a face full of freckles and a lopsided, mischievous grin. His most noticeable feature was a head of thick, blonde hair, which prompted his nickname, "Polar Bear." I don't think he found that nearly as amusing as his brothers and sisters did! Although he was undoubtedly one of the quietest members of our family, Henry was no stranger to bare-knuckle teasing, both at the receiving and doling out ends. Being part of the Friesen family was definitely a front-row ticket to being merciless teasing. One of my childhood memories involves being held on the floor by several brothers who tickled me until I screamed for mercy. The louder I screamed, the more satisfaction they got out of their shenanigans.

There were always new and better ways to torment a sister, especially one who was squeamish around creepy-crawly creatures. Henry had no fear of any kind of wildlife, and he took great delight in catching the emerald-striped garter snakes that slithered in the grass. My strong aversion to snakes triggered Henry's active imagination. He would chase me around the yard with a writhing snake in his clutches. When he managed to catch up with me, he would try to put the critter inside my shirt. It is not difficult to deduce where my over-the-top phobia of snakes came from. To this day, I react with a huge startle and a racing heart whenever I encounter a snake of any description.

Our farm always had an array of pets. We had the usual mixed-breed dog who barked at the approach of strangers, and occasionally, much to my dad's chagrin, chased after cars on the road. The barn was a haven for multiple cat families. Perhaps the most interesting pet we had was a colourful bantam rooster named Bennie. His unruly personality made up for his diminutive stature. His feathers were iridescent and changed colours with the fluctuating light. His undulating red comb crowned his little body, giving him a regal bearing. Bennie developed an unexplained attachment to Henry. Wherever Henry went, Bennie scampered after him. At the crack of dawn, Bennie managed to station himself under Henry's bedroom window and crow loudly to usher in a new day. There was no question where his loyalties lay.

Henry was not someone who blindly followed a predetermined path in life. His interests and hobbies defied the norm. While still in grade school, he and his cousin Sid raided a skunk's nest under an old abandoned house. I have no idea how they braved the odious scent of Mother Skunk, but they managed to sneak the little critters to our farm. They hired a veterinarian to surgically remove their scent sacs and sold them at a healthy profit to a pet store.

Another project the two adventurous entrepreneurs dreamed up was to convert an old granary into a hatchery, where they hatched pheasant eggs. Don't ask me where the eggs came from, but the end result was a pen of ring-necked pheasants. Their emerald-coloured heads and graceful bodies were an astounding and magnificent spectacle on an otherwise ordinary prairie farm. Other ventures included rescuing baby owls and crows. They fed them slices of stale bread mushed in warm milk.

As I mentioned, Henry was exceedingly quiet. At noisy, chatty family gatherings, he did not have much to say. He sat back and observed everyone else, his thoughts locked securely inside his mind. He did not seem particularly happy. I often wonder, as I look back, if I could have done more to draw him out, to explore what he was feeling, to ask him about how his life was going. But instead, I engaged with other family members who were eager to talk, or I busied myself in the kitchen preparing food or washing endless stacks of dishes.

In his mid-twenties, Henry married a lovely French girl from a neighbouring town. Her name was Linda and her long, black hair was in stark contrast to his blondeness. Although she was very quiet herself, she seemed to have the ability to draw him out of his introversion. I was proud to be a bridesmaid in their wedding party.

His entrepreneurship extended into his adult life. He developed a thriving construction business. With numerous employees working under him, he was involved in multiple construction projects. As quickly as a business can be built up from the ground, it can also fall apart. Henry's hard work collapsed around him as some of his prime customers were not able to meet their financial obligations. His lifetime dream was shattered, and along with it went his optimism and hope for a bright future. He sank into a deep depression that left him feeling defeated and hopeless. Ultimately, this desperate state of mind led to the breakup of his marriage. He drifted into a solitary existence, alone and shiftless.

Grace Tallman

The seat belt cinched my growing belly as the plane carried me and my developing baby westward. It had been four months since Dr. Graham revealed the startling news of my pregnancy. During these months, I had slept no more than two hours each night. Hour after anxious hour, I would lie awake, trying every technique I could think of. I listened to a tape of progressive relaxation exercises before bed, I avoided caffeine after lunch, I got regular physical exercise, walking to and from work each day. I don't know how I managed to keep up my rigorous schedule of going to work each day and doing all the tasks that accompany being a wife and mother, plus being pregnant.

Removed from my usual whirlwind of busyness, I suddenly had time to think and reflect. There were a lot of unanswered questions around Henry's death. What was the cause of death? How did it happen? Was he alone? Did someone call a doctor or an ambulance? How could everything have come to this chilling end?

I arrived in Winnipeg on the coldest night of the year. Having grown up there, it was no surprise to land in minus-thirty-five–degree weather. That was without the wind chill.

During my time in Manitoba, I stayed with my dad and stepmother. I prepared myself for another sleepless night as I crawled alone into the cold double bed. Devastating sadness, emptiness, along with unanswered questions played tag inside my mind as I drifted off to sleep. The next thing I remember was waking up with the morning sun streaming through the cracks in the blinds. I had slept throughout the entire night without waking up once. This seemed like a small miracle to me. I had not had a full night's sleep since I first became pregnant! The only conclusion I could come to was that the shock of Henry's death had jolted my sleeping mechanisms back to the default position.

Our large family rallied together and began searching for the missing pieces of the puzzle. In speaking to Linda and other members of the family who had had recent contact with Henry, it became apparent that his state of mind was one of hopelessness and despair when he was last seen alive. The physician who saw him in the emergency department raised suspicions that his death was not a result of "natural" causes. Suicide? The idea of Henry taking his own life was impossible for us to fathom. This was something that, until now, had never crossed our paths. This notion was later confirmed by the coroner's report: "Cause of death: arsenic poisoning."

Icy fingers of grief clutched my throat. My heart was raw with sorrow. Losing a brother to suicide carried heavy layers of sadness and guilt. My mind reeled with "what ifs" and "should haves." This was the tragedy that my mother had side-stepped with her death.

My mind returned to my present reality. All these vivid memories had been resurrected with Molly's question about my brother's suicide. The depression that tormented me came from the same demon that Henry succumbed to almost a year earlier. It was returning as if it intended to claim a second victim. In my attempts to bury my sorrow over Henry's death, I had managed to repress my grief. Now it was rearing its ugly head, invading my psyche, dragging me relentlessly into the clutches of depression and thoughts of suicide.

Life on the Psychiatric Ward

Sometimes even to live is an act of courage.
—Seneca

The mattress and pillow on my bed were sheathed in protective plastic. They were hot and uncomfortable. The front of my room consisted of a large window that faced directly onto the nursing station that was enclosed by glass. I was placed on suicide watch. Every fifteen minutes during the night, a nurse entered my room and shone a flashlight to check that I was breathing and safe.

My emotions continued to feel like a whirlwind inside of me. Part of me felt relief that I was finally getting help for my depression. Another part of me felt cautious and reluctant to give up the fierce struggle that had kept me alive for the past few months. I felt like I was relinquishing control, like I was falling backward, not knowing whether anyone would be there to catch me.

The very next morning, I was introduced to Dr. Walton, who would be the psychiatrist in charge of my care while I was in the hospital. I felt instantly at ease with him. He was soft spoken, with a calm, gentle manner. He asked me all the questions that he needed to formulate a professional opinion of my mental state. His attitude was respectful, and for some reason, I felt in awe that I was being taken seriously. Without fully realizing it, I was waiting for someone to say, "Just snap out of it!" because that was the self-talk that was roiling around in my brain. I was feeling a great deal of stigma, guilt, and shame for what was happening in my life. The critical voice inside my head was telling me that I should be at home with my husband and children, fulfilling my role as a wife and mother. I felt that I was neglecting my family. Was I just being lazy and self-indulgent? Did I have the right to focus on my own needs at the expense of those who depended on me?

Dr. Walton was quick to assure me that my reasons for being at the hospital were completely legitimate. He informed me that I was suffering from severe postpartum depression. I developed an instant positive rapport and trust in him and agreed to his plan to treat the depression with antidepressant medication. Taking medications involved suffering through the inevitable side effects that initially accompanied the treatment—grogginess, and feeling detached and spaced out. I was told that it could take up to one month before the positive effects would begin to outweigh the downside of the medications. It took several attempts to find a combination of drugs that was effective and whose side effects I could live with.

Being a voracious reader, I gravitated to the library at the hospital and borrowed every book I could find on the topic of my illness. There was a lot of information on major depression, but a limited amount on postpartum depression. Every book I read seemed to concur that vigorous physical exercise was one of the best adjunctive ways of helping yourself through depression. I was on board with this advice! Exercise had always been a vital way for me to cope with all that life threw at me. Through exercise, I could gain back some control in my recovery.

I lost no time in hopping on the stationary bicycle in the patient lounge. I pedaled vigorously. My inner voices urged me to go faster, harder, longer. It dawned on me that I was using only my lower body muscles, so I incorporated energetic arm movements. The books said "vigorous," didn't they? Once I completed my thirty minutes on the bike, I retreated to my room, pulled out my yoga mat, and crunched out sit-ups and leg raises. My goal was 200 sit-ups a day. Ironically, while my mental health was suffering, I became more physically fit than I had ever been.

A few days after my admission, I met a woman who would be another strong force on my journey to recovery.

"Hi, Grace," she greeted me in a cheerful voice as she sat down next to me on the bed. "My name is Sue. I will be your social worker while you are here."

It did not take long for me to feel that I had another advocate, someone who understood my situation. I did not need to explain anything to her. Her long-standing employment in the mental health field gave her inside knowledge about what I was experiencing. That morning was the first of a long series of conversations between us that would prove to be a source of hope and strength for me.

Sue intuitively recognized that a significant factor in my depression was the tension between myself and Bruce. We were like two ships passing each other at night, like two sets of railway tracks that ran parallel to each other without ever connecting. I had not been able to resolve my feelings of abandonment from the previous summer when Bruce left me and Alana on our own. There were many unspoken feelings of resentment between us. Until my hospital admission, I had assumed the majority of the burden of childcare and household chores. Now that I was in the hospital, he was saddled with all the responsibility. I felt incredibly guilty while realizing that there was nothing I could do about it until I regained my stability. The mountain of tension and bitterness between us felt insurmountable. I was at the point of considering ending our marriage.

Sue wasn't so sure. She felt that our marital relationship was an essential element in the framework of my mental health. It was her suggestion that we try couple counselling. My immediate response was reluctance. My hopes had been dashed on the shores of recent life experiences. Sue was like a dog with a bone and kept suggesting that we at least try it out. Sue's persistence finally convinced me that my mental health would improve significantly if we could mend the gaping tear in the fabric of our marriage.

Bruce was not enthused with the idea. He had not had the opportunity to develop a trusting relationship with Sue the way I had. I think it was with a measure of resistance that he finally agreed to participate. Every Wednesday afternoon,

Bruce showed up at the hospital and, with Sue's guidance, we struggled to bridge the gap that loomed between us. I think these sessions were very painful for Bruce, because he felt like Sue and I were ganging up on him. Eventually, Jeremy, the hospital chaplain, joined our sessions so that Bruce would feel represented, as well. The counselling provided the glue that helped us stick together for the time being.

The Road to Recovery

You were strong enough to get this far.
You are strong enough to keep going.
—Anonymous

Depression is not an illness that you get over in a hurry. It was a series of trials and errors with different medications. The four weeks that had been estimated for the alleviation of my symptoms turned into almost four months. I met almost every day with Dr. Walton. I continued to be an active partner in my recovery by keeping careful records of my moods and medication changes, and of course, vigorous exercise. During my stay at the hospital, Dr. Walton granted me weekly evening passes to attend aerobics-instructor classes at the downtown YMCA. It had been a long-time dream of mine to become a fitness instructor. I was taking my commitment to being physically fit to a new level. I was resolved to maximize every opportunity of self-determination on my journey to recovery.

I attended weekly group classes where I learned practical ways of coping with the symptoms of mental illness. The classes were facilitated by hospital staff, and each week, we were given homework assignments to practice these new skills in our daily lives.

I learned how to become aware of difficult emotions and ways of dealing with these feelings constructively, rather than acting impulsively.

I learned how to self-soothe when things felt out of control and to find helpful ways of handling challenging situations. I was taught to focus on the present moment and attend to what was happening in the here and now in a calm way. It is amazing how much easier it is to deal with life when you focus on one circumstance at a time.

I learned to become more effective in my interpersonal relationships, becoming aware of my needs and wishes and communicating them in ways that were respectful both to myself and the other person. All of these skills were a repetition of what I had learned in my training to become a chaplain.

Integrating new ways of living only comes with daily persistence and commitment. I felt empowered as I slowly but surely absorbed these skills and tried to incorporate them into my life.

Gradually, little by little, my mood became stable. I began to see life in a positive light again. Bruce and I had reclaimed our marriage. We began communicating our thoughts and feelings to each other in a clear and regular way. The many hours and the conscious efforts we applied to making our relationship work paid off with very positive dividends.

After almost forty-two years, our relationship is thriving and growing stronger every day. I am so grateful to Sue for persisting in her efforts to help us rebuild our relationship.

After being discharged from the hospital, I returned to my role as a mother and wife. I continued to see Sue on a weekly outpatient basis. Her ongoing presence in my life helped tremendously with the transition back into the community.

Eventually, I was able to return to work, but I made it a priority to cut back my hours to a part-time status. I would always continue to be aware of my vulnerability. I knew from experience that pacing myself would be a practice that could never be allowed to fall by the wayside again.

I gradually became adept at being more assertive and clear about my needs. I learned that speaking out and expressing what I need is not selfish; it is foundational for mental health and wellness. Assertiveness is a way to gain both self-respect and the respect of others.

Like a broken bone that has healed, the point of injury is stronger than before. It will never be broken in the same place again. I gained a deepened sense of empathy for people who struggled in their lives. Depression is not a permanent state, although it certainly feels that way while you are in the thick of it. There is an end to the suffering, but there is no guarantee just how long you will have to wait.

❦

More than twenty years later, I am thriving. I feel fulfilled in my professional and personal life. I am wiser and more resilient than before. I am more conscious of my inner strength. I am a lifelong survivor. All the stepping stones on my journey have made me who I am today. Looking back, I don't know if I would change any of my experiences, even though some of them have been more painful than I could have imagined. I have learned, through my experience, the truth of the maxim, "What doesn't kill you, makes you stronger."

Epilogue

Perhaps you will not be surprised to learn that I am now working as a mental health counsellor with a local community agency. When the opportunity presents itself, I draw upon my own experience with depression to offer hope and support to clients who are feeling hopeless and adrift. I can assure them that there is a way through even the darkest times in life.

Our three children have become established as adults. We are so proud of each of them! Hailey graduated with a master's degree in art therapy. She is working successfully as an art therapist in London and we enjoy her company frequently for Sunday dinners. Brandon has migrated to the beauty of Canada's West Coast, where he owns a landscaping company. What more perfect location could you find than Victoria, BC, to enjoy this field of work? Too bad he is so far away. We would love to see more of him.

Can you believe, our youngest, Alana, turned twenty-five a few days ago? In some ways, she grew up as an only child, because her siblings were so much older than her. Her intelligence has always been very evident from the encyclopedic store of knowledge she demonstrated. When asked a question, she would respond in great detail, extrapolating every possible angle. I have always been in complete awe at the vastness of her knowledge. She excelled in her schoolwork and was always at the top of her class. She had a small group of friends to whom she devoted her loyalty. I recall making breakfast on many Saturday mornings for her and four of her friends after a sleepover (a giggle-over might be more accurate). She followed in her sister's footsteps in pursuing her artistic talents. She enrolled in a two-year art program at the high school she attended. She produced an amazing array of artwork, including an anatomically correct drawing. With a mind that was so oriented to detail, she decided to pursue a science degree. She is currently completing her zoology degree at the University of Guelph.

*

I arranged to take Alana out for lunch on her twenty-fifth birthday. The beautiful May morning was bathed in sunshine. The sky overhead was cloudless. Tulips, daffodils, and hyacinths bloomed in bursts of astonishing colour. Despite the noise of busy noon traffic, my ears perked up as I heard a robin trilling its cheerful song in the tree just outside the restaurant. Over our salads, I took the opportunity to tell Alana how much I loved her—that my love for her had saved both of our lives so many years earlier. I assured her that, even though my pregnancy with her was totally unexpected and unplanned, I had never called it a mistake. It was definitely a surprise—a beautiful, wonderful gift that continues to give me pride and joy.

As I prepared to get back in my car to drive home, Alana gave me one of her signature hugs, a "crack-every-rib-in-your-chest hug." Tears streamed down our cheeks. They were not tears of sadness; they were tears of connection and happiness. I took a step back and looked at my youngest daughter, who was now so grown up and capable. I saw the blueness of the sky reflected in her beautiful eyes.

I realized that I was happy—very, very happy.

Dear Pain,

*I think we both underestimated each other.
I underestimated your perseverance, your nuclear force to overwhelm me, and your unbroken willingness to have a place in my life.
But you underestimated my tenacity, too.*

*Sincerely yours,
Hanging in There*

My brother Henry on his wedding day, 1976

Bruce and Grace, July 1976

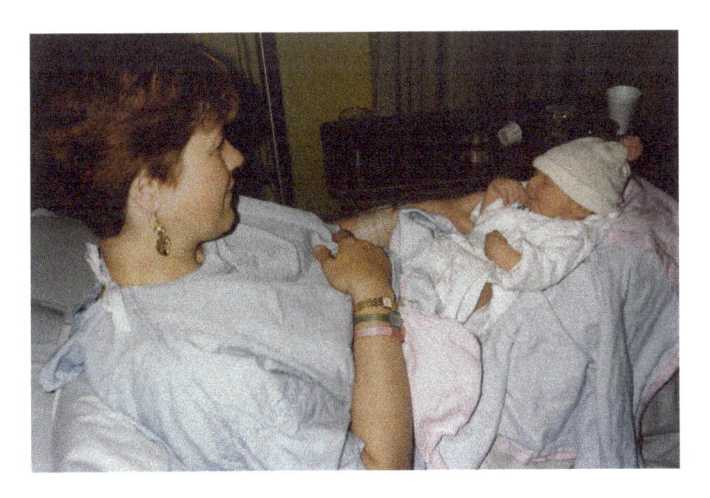

Grace and Alana, half an hour after her birth

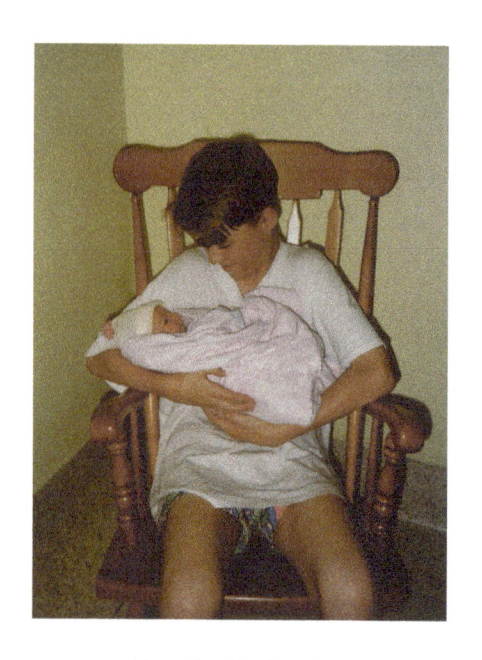

Proud brother Brandon

Grace, Bruce & Alana

Bruce reading to Alana

Big sister Hailey with Alana

Hailey, Brandon and Alana

Grace & Alana, September, 2018

PART TWO:
Paths To Resilience

What is Resilience?

I am sitting at my computer as I am writing this. All the windows in my house are open, allowing the fresh summer air to waft in. Over the past few weeks, the air inside has grown stale and a little musty with days of temperatures in the mid-to-high thirties. The air conditioner has been labouring endlessly in a vain effort to keep the temperatures at a comfortable level.

My freshly washed laundry is fluttering on the line in the gentle summer breeze. In the background, I hear a plethora of summer sounds: traffic hurrying by on the busy street nearby, motorcycles sounding like crazed mosquitoes as they rev their engines. Just outside my window, I hear the gentler sounds of cicadas making their first appearance of the season and birds softly twittering as they land on my bird feeder. My garden is happy and thriving, freshly watered from a lovely rain a few days ago that broke the heat wave.

It seems like a natural environment in which to talk about resilience. I wonder if it would be a more difficult subject to broach if a storm was hovering on the horizon or if the yard was covered in three-foot snow drifts.

I was initially introduced to the concept of resilience in my Psychology 101 class. The professor posed the following scenario: "Two sisters in the same family go through identical difficulties. One of the sisters not only survives, but thrives, despite the challenges; the other one becomes totally overwhelmed and lives a life filled with hopelessness and disappointment. What makes the difference in these two women who share the same DNA and life experience?"

The question was a rhetorical one, but it sparked an eager fascination within me. The answer, of course, was: Resilience. This inspired me to embark on a quest to study the concept of resilience. I began to passionately look for books on the topic. I ransacked the local library and borrowed every book that I could find with the word "resilient" in the title, or as part of the subject matter. I ordered books from the internet and began to build a miniature library with volumes on resilience. Every morning began with at least an hour of studying about the subject. I entered extensive notes and quotations into my journal. I read real-life accounts of people who had persevered through various hardships and emerged even stronger than before.

I was particularly fascinated by the research that has been conducted on post-traumatic growth by Richard Tedeschi and Lawrence Calhoun at the University of North Carolina. Through scientific analysis, they have discovered that up to sixty percent of people who suffer trauma go on to lead productive and resilient lives without developing full-blown PTSD. Although they experience many of the symptoms of PTSD—such as flashbacks, intrusive thoughts, nightmares, and depression—they simultaneously recognize that their struggle to survive unleashes their strengths. People who have experienced post-traumatic growth report the following changes in their lives:

1. My priorities have changed. I am not afraid to do what makes me happy.
2. I feel closer to my friends and family.
3. I understand myself better. I know who I really am now.
4. I have a new sense of purpose and meaning in my life.
5. I am better able to focus on my dreams and goals.

That brings me to the question: "What is resilience?"

A dictionary definition is "an ability to recover from or adjust easily to misfortune or change." I believe that the phrase "adjust easily" is a misnomer, because resilience is not necessarily easy. I have heard resilience compared to snapping an elastic band; as soon as you release the tension, it springs back to its original form. Again, this implies that resilience is an immediate response to hardship, which is definitely not the case. People do not adjust easily or spring back from adversity in a split second.

The simplest definition I have heard for resilience is: "The courage to face things that are hard for us." This one is from Jane McGonigal, author of *Superbetter*. The book chronicles her difficult struggle after a debilitating concussion and is one of the books about resilience that impacted me most profoundly.

A. Principles Of Resilience

I will outline some of the basic principles of resilience that I have gleaned from intensive self-study on the topic. In addition, everything I have to say about resilience has been filtered through my own personal experience, and I can vouch for the fact that I found it to be helpful in my own life. Before I continue any further, I want to say that the road to resilience, which I will be talking about in the upcoming chapters, applies to people with mild-to-moderate depression or to anyone who is simply wanting to cope in a healthier way with life's adversities.

Anyone who is feeling severely depressed with any thoughts of suicide needs to seek immediate help by contacting a medical doctor or a mental health counsellor. In collaboration with your family physician, you will be guided in pursuing the most suitable intervention and support that you need at this time. Under no circumstances should you ignore your symptoms. Depression is a legitimate illness that benefits from appropriate treatment in the same way as diabetes or appendicitis.

1. Everyone Can Build Resilience

We are all born with a certain amount of resilience. We would not survive if we did not possess some degree of it. Even the gruelling process of being born requires that we be able to bounce back. Enduring the labour process and being squeezed through a tiny birth canal is an extremely challenging way to start your journey of life, if you stop and reflect on it.

However, the amount of resilience we end up with in our individual lives is not fixed; in fact, it varies considerably from one individual to the next. As in my psychology professor's example , two highly similar individuals can respond very differently to trying circumstances. The question that continues to plague me is: Why did I survive my struggle with depression but my brother Henry did not? I am consumed with grief when I think of the mental anguish he must have gone through that ultimately led to his suicide.

Although building resilience in the face of traumatic experiences is a possibility for everyone, the tragedy remains that, for some, the ability to reach out for help seems impossible. In the absence of a viable lifeline at a crucial crossroad in their life, they simply find themselves unable to go on. Strong family and social networks are key factors in building resilience, and when these are absent, the result can be overwhelming. Unfortunately, Henry had become isolated in his life and lacked a solid source of social connection at the time of his death. His low self-esteem, his depression, and his inability to reach out for the help he needed resulted in tragedy.

Building greater resilience takes time, effort, commitment, and focus. It does not happen to you overnight, and it cannot be learned from reading a book. Resilience needs to be developed in the real trenches of your life. It's a process that will take months to learn and master. Don't be frustrated by this, because unlike your eye colour or height, resilience is not a trait but a skill that you can readily enhance with patience and training.

2. You Are Stronger than You Think

All of us have already overcome many difficulties and struggles in our lives. Life is not a cake walk for anybody. If you look back over your life, ask yourself: What have I achieved? What have I conquered? We all tend to diminish our own accomplishments. We are tempted to look at other people and become envious of their abilities and strengths; meanwhile, those very individuals may be looking at us with the same thoughts.

Not only do we minimize our strengths, we maximize our failings and inadequacies. This is a form of cognitive distortion that can have crippling effects. For example, I have presented workshops and facilitated many grief support groups that have generated very positive evaluations. However, one minor negative comment can influence my whole perception about the success of what I accomplished. If I allow myself to, I can become totally focused on that one unfavourable comment and feel like I have failed. On the other hand, how often have you received a compliment for something you accomplished and immediately downplayed it by belittling what you did? Somebody was recognizing your strength, but you unconsciously minimized it and refused to acknowledge that what you had just achieved was amazing.

All too often when we are facing a challenge, we focus on our weaknesses rather than our strengths. And yet, everybody, without exception, possesses strengths that make them a unique and resilient individual. Knowing what your strengths are can make the difference between being engulfed by life's challenges and thriving.

I encourage you to visit the VIA Institute on Character website and take the following test that help you to determine what your unique strengths are:

http://www.viacharacter.org/www/Character-Strengths. Discover the areas of life in which you shine. Use the qualities that come most naturally to you to improve your life and begin thriving.

Acknowledge your strengths and use them daily. Throw aside any sense of false modesty. Jane McGonigal, in her book about resilience, suggests that you come up with a nickname to call yourself based on your five character strengths. My nickname is "Grace the Compassionate One." I'm sure you can come with something that describes you equally well. Dare to be creative, stick your neck out, and capitalize on the strong points that you identify as your character strengths on the test. Stop focusing on all the things that limit you and start celebrating your strengths, abilities, and achievements.

3. Life is Not Fair, But Life is Good

How many times have you heard someone cry out in protest, "It's not fair!"? This is usually in response to a negative event occurring in the individual's life that seems totally disproportionate to what they expected. Well, guess what? Life is NOT fair. Unfairness abounds in our world. Some blatant, recent examples of this include the volcano in Guatemala, the earthquake in Mexico, and the unrelenting war in the Middle East that has resulted in an unprecedented number of displaced people. On a regular basis, people who do not deserve it, suffer. I have told you the story of my mother's suffering. She was the kindest, most saintly person you could ever meet, and she experienced many bouts of cancer throughout her life. She definitely did not deserve the painful death she endured.

I recall a memorable lecture given by a hospital chaplain when I was a nursing student. He addressed our class to give us some insight into his role on the medical team of a large inner-city hospital. He witnessed tragedy on a daily basis in the form of devastating illness and injury of his patients. He told us that often people would turn to him and ask a question to which there was no easy answer: "Why is this happening to me?" His comeback to the question initially shocked me. His answer was simply, "Why NOT you?"

After reflecting on this, I realized the truth in what he said. There is no question that, in our world, good people suffer, and evil people's actions go unpunished. Why should anyone feel that they should be spared when others around them suffer unfairly?

The other side of the coin, about life not being fair, is the incontrovertible thought that life is still good. Somehow, we need to believe that the world is not a hostile place, that good is always foundational, and that evil is secondary to it. I suppose this would be called optimism, which is a character trait that I inherited from my dad. As a result of my gene pool, I recognize that it might be easier for me to take this stance than it is for others. Am I hiding my head in the sand?

No, I don't think I'm being an ostrich. In the words of Noam Chomsky, in his book *Manufacturing Consent,* "Optimism is a strategy for making a better future. Because unless you believe that the future can be better, you are unlikely to step up and take responsibility for making it so."

We will never fully understand how the universe works because it is so immense and complex. However, we can choose to decide that it is benevolent and learn to move forward with our lives with joy and confidence.

4. Resilience is the Result of Hundreds of Tiny Steps

Life is a marathon, not a sprint. Every little success helps you gain confidence for the next step. Research in the field of positive psychology has shown that many seemingly insignificant successes or victories have a greater impact on resilience than one major success. That is why it is so important to manage your life by taking frequent baby steps. Have you ever watched a young child taking their first steps? The first move in the journey to mobility is to learn to crawl. Next, they learn to pull themselves up on a piece of furniture, then they start moving along while holding onto a wall or a parent's hand. Gradually, the parents encourage the child to hang onto just their baby finger. The final stage is when the child completely lets go of all supports and takes the first few steps independently; tottering and tentative, initially, but before you know it, the parents can hardly keep up with them as they race around the house.

What tiny little thing can I do today that would make me happier, stronger, braver?

Make it your goal to take small steps every day toward your goals or values, even when it is difficult for you.

5. We're All in This Together

As I have already mentioned several times, it is important to realize that we all struggle and face hardships. It is part of our human condition. Nobody is exempt from wrestling with the difficulties in life. We all have stress and challenges in our personal lives, at work, in relationships, and in our lives, in general. We will all, at some point, lose someone we love. Some people are really good at disguising their struggles and putting up a facade that seems to say, "Look at me! My life is perfect!"

"Nobody is perfect. Everybody suffers. If you can accept your suffering, then you will understand other people better. Be grateful for pain. Love life." This is a quote from Stephen Colbert, who makes a living from making people laugh on his Comedy Central show.

B. Steps To Building Resilience

In the ensuing pages, I will share some practical strategies for developing resilience. These steps are simple and accessible to everyone who chooses to avail themselves of them. I am sharing the journey that worked for me. There is no cookie-cutter approach to building resilience. Each of the steps that I took can be modified to meet the needs of your own journey.

A bank account can be used as a metaphor for building resilience. There will always be expenses to pay, such as the rent or mortgage, hydroelectricity, and taxes. Just when we think we are finally caught up with all the payments, something unanticipated will come up, such as a leaky roof or a broken kitchen faucet. In a similar way, every life has a withdrawal and a deposit column. Withdrawals in life are things such as illness, disappointments, failures, deaths of loved ones. Many of these situations are out of our control. No matter how hard we work at it, we will never be able to eliminate the debits on the left side of the ledger. What we have more control of are the deposits, or the resilience-building steps we take in our life. Our goal is to make more deposits than withdrawals to maintain a positive balance.

1. Be Connected

I truly believe that a sense of connectedness is the key ingredient to building resilience. As I stated in the Principles of Resilience, "We're all in this together." In the darkest hour of my life, I reached out to someone I trusted, my family doctor.

Unfortunately, the lack of ability to reach out is one of the debilitating symptoms of depression. This was the case with my brother Henry. The isolation that so often accompanies depression reminds me of the kind of bacteria that thrive in dark, damp places like old running shoes. As long as they remain hidden from the light, these bacteria flourish and multiply. Exposure to sunlight is the last thing these virulent microorganisms can tolerate. In the case of depression, exposure to the warmth of connection to a caring human being can be life-altering. Reaching out to a friend or family member you trust, even if it is just a feeble, split-second cry for help, can make all the difference. Perhaps the person you reach out to will be the link in the chain that can put you in touch with the help that you need most.

The importance of human connection was clearly demonstrated in the well-known Grant & Glueck study from Harvard University. The study kept track of the lives of 268 male graduates from Harvard as well as 456 poor men who grew up in Boston from 1939 to 2014. The current director of the study, Robert Waldinger, says, "The warmth of relationships throughout life has the greatest impact on life satisfaction." He goes on to say, "It's not just the number of friends you have, and it's not whether you are in a committed relationship. It's the quality of your close relationships that matters." More information can be found at the following web page:

https://www.cnbc.com/2016/12/15/75-year-harvard-study-reveals-the-key-to-success-in-2017-and-beyond.html.

Since human connection is so important, what are some ways of cultivating it? Extroverts love to surround themselves with large groups of friends and acquaintances, but what about introverts like myself? I find that simple acts of thoughtfulness and kindness can go a long way in improving the quality of relationships. How about sending a thank-you card or an email to a friend who has done something for you? So often we wait for someone else to reach out to us. Be willing to step beyond your comfort zone. Take a risk and be the first one to reach out and connect.

An exercise that was recommended in a book that I read recently was to connect with someone in your life who really inspired you or helped you get through a difficult time in the past. Perhaps it was a teacher, a neighbour, or a minister who touched your life in a significant way. It doesn't matter how long ago it was, the internet has many ways of helping you find people who mattered to you, even if it was many years ago.

Something as simple as a smile can have far-reaching effects. Have you ever had the experience of a complete stranger giving you a bright smile as they walked by? For a brief moment, your heart feels lighter and you feel a connection to someone you have never seen before and probably will never see again. This has a contagious effect; you are more likely to feel inclined to smile at the next person you meet.

Treat the clerk at the grocery store with kindness. Thank them for their work, ask them about their life. Call them by the name on their name tag. Your efforts at connection give you instant rewards of gratification and a boost in your own mood.

Connection is not reserved for humans. Four-legged friends can have a very positive effect on helping people overcome difficult life experiences. The National Institute of Mental Health recognizes pet therapy as a legitimate treatment for mental illnesses such as depression, PTSD, and autism.

2. Develop Positive Attitudes and Beliefs

Have you ever considered what an important role your attitude and beliefs or thoughts play in the way you experience life? A quote from Aldous Huxley may illuminate this question to some degree: "It is not what happens to you; it's what you do with what happens to you."

"Research has demonstrated that the number-one roadblock to resilience is our thinking style," writes Karen Reivich in her book, *The Resilience Factor*. Pay attention to what are you thinking when you're not thinking about anything. What habitual thoughts occupy your mind? What kind of a conversation are you holding with yourself?

Your attitude and beliefs affect the quality of everything you do. For example, if your attitude is full of negativity and resistance you will always struggle in facing the difficulties in your life.

A very effective strategy for building a more positive outlook in life is to develop an attitude of gratitude. Something that has worked for me is to pause for a few minutes every night before I go to sleep. I reflect back on the day and express appreciation for everything positive that happened in the past twenty-four hours. I have a small, smooth white stone that I hold in my hand as I reflect on the blessings of the day that has just passed. The stone is a tangible reminder to focus my mind on all the things for which I am grateful. At the top of my list, I usually include my family, the wonderful, peaceful country we live in, as well as my overall good health. It is amazing how thoughts of small gratitudes start tumbling into your mind as you open yourself to this possibility. It is virtually impossible to feel grateful and despondent at the same time. "It is not joy that makes us grateful. It is gratitude that makes us joyful," according to Brother David Steindl-Rast in his book, *Words of Common Sense for Mind, Body and Soul*.

A positive attitude can be described at three different levels. The basic level is hope. Hopefulness is an attitude that will move you in the direction of a resilient outlook. Hope is believing that a good outcome is POSSIBLE. The ability to imagine a good outcome is indicative of hope.

Optimism goes a step further. Not only does an optimist believe that a good outcome is possible, but that it is LIKELY. Optimism helps individuals reach for bigger and higher goals. Optimism is a great motivator.

The third and most developed positive attitude is self-efficacy. This is the belief that a positive result is not only possible and likely, but that it is within YOUR CONTROL to achieve. It is the belief that your efforts at improving your situation will succeed.

In my own life, my faith in a Higher Power has always sustained me in difficult times. Having grown up in a deeply devout family, it is totally natural for me to continue to find solace and strength in my spiritual beliefs.

3. Self-Care

Rest, relaxation, nutrition, and exercise: these are the foundations of self-care. It has to start there. This is basic survival; resilience is not even an option until your basic needs are being met. It is surprising how many clients I encounter in my work as a mental health counsellor who do not practice adequate self-care. My purpose in writing this chapter is not a "how-to" manual on taking care of yourself, but simply to raise the awareness of its significance.

Sleep

Sleep and relaxation are as important to our health as eating, drinking, and breathing. It allows our body to repair itself and our brain to rejuvenate. Allow enough time in your daily schedule to get adequate sleep. It is crucial to slow down the pace of your life sufficiently to take care of what is most important. If it means saying no to non-essential requests, then that's what you need to do. Insomnia is a modern-day epidemic. I am not an expert in this matter, but if you feel that this is an area that you would like more help with, I would recommend that you discuss it with your family doctor. I have also found the following website from Harvard Medical School to be a helpful resource:

https://www.health.harvard.edu/newsletter_article/sleep-and-mental-health.

Nutrition

Nutrition is a very personal choice, and there are as many food preferences, restrictions, and fads as there are individuals. Whatever choices you make in your dietary practices, make sure you research the evidence in order to make sound ones.

Depression can have a powerful influence on your eating habits. It can either cause an increase or a decrease in your appetite. In my case, I definitely experienced a sharp decline in my appetite and I completely lost interest in eating. If not eating enough is a concern, try and eat a small amount every couple of hours. I encourage my clients to take care of their own basic needs in the same way they would care for a small baby or a defenceless pet. You would never consider depriving those who depend on you of their most basic needs. Why not nurture yourself in the same compassionate way? If you do not look after yourself, who will?

If, on the other hand, you tend to overeat, try and discover what the underlying motivations are for this behaviour. Often eating more than you want or need is based on unmet emotional needs. Rather than going on fad diets, consider going for counseling to better understand what is going on in your life. Cognitive behavioural therapy can have very effective results, not only in losing weight, but also in gaining insight into your emotional responses to the issues in your life.

Exercise

From reading my story, I'm sure you have gathered that exercise was a huge part of my recovery. To this day, I continue to reap the positive effects of exercise in my life. Just a few days ago, after a long day at work, I was feeling tired and slightly melancholy. I was tempted to lie down in my bed and take a quick nap. I recalled how exercise had always been regenerative for me in the past, so instead, I laced up my running shoes and went on a brisk forty-five-minute walk. When I returned I felt renewed, both physically and emotionally.

Scientific research has clearly demonstrated that exercise is an effective treatment for mild-to-moderate depression. The positive effects of exercise on mood and energy are related to the chemicals that are released in your body when you exercise. These chemicals, called endorphins, stimulate a positive feeling in your brain that is similar to that produced by taking morphine.

Exercise can also help you feel better because it is a positive distraction from the cycles of negative thinking that you can become trapped in.

One of my clients developed symptoms of severe depression following the death of her husband. She was started on an antidepressant, but her low mood was unrelenting. She was determined to find a way to feel better. She took out a gym membership and hired a personal trainer. The only time she was able to find relief from her depression was while she was working out. She says it also really helped that her trainer was cute! Month after month, three times a week, she made her way to the gym. There were days when she had to brush several feet of snow off her car in order to go, but she maintained her commitment. Her commitment to exercise made the difference between debilitating depression and her gradual recovery to mental wellness.

The question is: How does one cope with hopelessness and lack of energy and still find the motivation to exercise? How do I get started and stay motivated? Starting and sticking with an exercise routine can be a real challenge. Here are some suggestions that may be helpful:

Recognize that even a small amount of exercise is better than nothing at all. Even five or ten minutes of moving your body will benefit. Start with whatever you can commit yourself to, and gradually increase the amount of time you spend.

Discover what you enjoy doing. I have engaged in different types of exercise over the course of my life: swimming, cycling, aerobics classes. I have never been a runner, but my current activity is simply brisk walking. I have purchased a Fitbit, which is very motivating. I attempt to walk 10,000 steps, per day, at least four or five times a week. Most phones come with some kind of pedometer, so you don't have to spend money on any expensive tracking gadgets.

Don't think of exercise as a chore. Try and view it as a way of helping yourself become healthier—physically and mentally. Look at it as a gift you give yourself.

Set your own personal goals. Make your goals reasonable, but also be willing to challenge yourself a little.

Try and determine what holds you back from achieving your exercise goals. If you lack motivation, it might be helpful to find a partner who will join you in your activity.

Whatever form of exercise you choose, do it regularly. Make it a part of your daily routine.

Many people have reported a boost in self-confidence and self-esteem as a result of regular exercise. It can help with weight loss and a positive self-image. The tangible gains you achieve from whatever routine you decide on will be motivating in themselves and be an incentive to keep going.

Self-Affirmation

The goal of resilient thinking is not to have optimistic or happy thoughts all of the time. Accuracy is more significant than optimism. For example, there was a time during my depression when I thought I would never feel happy again.

This was a debilitating thought that is prevalent in people who suffer from depression. It would be futile to go from thinking *I will never feel happy again* to *I feel great!* A more accurate assessment of my situation would have been to say, "With time, I will start to feel better if I continue to work with my doctor, take my prescribed medications, and participate in doing what I have been told will be helpful."

See what happens when you say the following affirmations to yourself. You can read them quietly or say them out loud in front of a mirror:

- *I accept myself as I am.*
- *I am strong today.*
- *I forgive myself.*
- *Whatever happens, I will be OK.*
- *I did everything I could today.*
- *Just for today, I don't need to fix or change anything.*

Self-Compassion

A vital part of self-care that we often overlook is our ability to practice self-compassion. Why is it that we sometimes care more about someone else than we care about ourselves? So often we are self-critical and harsh with ourselves, especially when we don't meet the sometimes unrealistic expectations we have placed on ourselves. Social media can have the effect of making us feel like we are the only one whose life is not perfect. You can be the most loving and understanding person, but if your compassion does not include yourself, it is incomplete.

I recently discovered an amazing author named Kristen Neff. She studied self-compassion as part of her doctoral research and currently teaches at the University of Texas in Austin. She wrote a book called *Self Compassion* as well as a companion workbook on the topic. She is passionate about spreading the word about being compassionate toward yourself. She has designed a self-test that you can take online to assess your level of self-compassion. The test is helpful, both in determining how self-compassionate you are, as well as pointing out ways in which you might be self-sabotaging by being harsh with yourself. I encourage you to go to the following link if you are interested in learning more about self-compassion: http://self-compassion.org/test-how-self-compassionate-you-are/.

In her book *You Can Heal Yourself*, Louise L. Hay offers some timeless advice about self-compassion: "You've been criticising yourself for years and it hasn't worked. Try approving of yourself and see what happens."

4. Learn from Nature

Taking the time to stop and observe nature has been a vital part of my journey to recovery. I reflect back on the time when I was a young mother with two small children to look after. The housework, cooking, diaper-changing, and wiping of runny noses could become overwhelming and all-consuming. I remember making a concerted effort to ensure that I took the children out of the house on a daily basis to take in some fresh air. Even in the winter, when just getting dressed in snowsuits, boots, scarves, and mittens seemed like a daunting task, we managed to get outdoors. Somehow, the vastness of the sky, the freshness in the air, and the birds singing in the treetops gave me pause to look at life with renewed eyes.

Nature has taught me many valuable, uplifting lessons. Take for example the changing of the seasons. Year after year, without fail, spring, summer, fall, and winter follow each other in regular succession. No matter how brutal the winter has been, it cannot prevent the spring from bringing its warmth and the beginning of new life. In a similar fashion, every morning the sun rises in the eastern sky, breathing the promise of light to another day. . Somehow, this provides me with a feeling of constancy and predictability in an otherwise chaotic universe.

On a cloudy day, no matter how dark and grey the sky may be, we know that the sun is still there, it just isn't clearly visible. Have you ever flown in a plane on a cloudy day, when the sky is completely overcast? As the plane rises in the air, suddenly, you are above the bank of clouds, and the sun comes back into view. You realize that it was there all the time; you just couldn't see it.

What about that hot, humid summer day that finally is cleansed with a refreshing thunderstorm? When the sun eventually re-emerges from the storm, the sky is arced with the iridescence of a brilliant rainbow. Every time this happens, my breath gets caught in my throat. At a moment like this, I am in awe of the unparalleled artistry of the Master Creator.

Throughout this book, I have talked about my strong affinity for birds. Whenever I am outdoors, my ears are always tuned to hear their beautiful songs. I once watched a movie about World War II. In the midst of the pandemonium and chaos of guns and bombs, I noticed that, in the background, the birds carried on with their usual lives. No matter what devastation happens around them, the birds still sing.

Nature has many more lessons to teach us about resilience. Perhaps the few examples I have mentioned here will inspire you to become more reflective of the natural world around you.

5. Live in the Moment

Part of practicing mindfulness is living in the present moment. It is the act of focusing on one thing at a time—each breath you take, each step as you walk, the sights and sounds around you. You probably have heard the phrase, "Be in the zone." This means being so absorbed with what you are doing that you forget about everything else around you in that moment.

One way of savouring the present moment is to activate your five senses. I call this the "Five by Five Exercise." It consists of simply engaging each of your five senses in five different ways. This is a powerful exercise. It doesn't cost a penny and all it takes is the active use of your imagination. The instructions are straightforward and easy, but the results are powerful. Here's what you do:

- Grab a notebook or paper and a pen (it is most effective if you write down your thoughts as you think of them).
- List your five senses and, under each sense, write five things that give you joy when using that part of your consciousness.

- To help you get started, I have shared some of my own examples. After reading what I have written, write your own responses.

The Five Senses

1. Sight
    - *Red cardinals.*
    - *Rainbows after a storm.*
    - *Sunrise or sunset.*
    - *Flowers, especially red roses.*
    - *Cat curled up on a window sill sleeping in the sun.*

2. Sound
    - *Birds singing.*
    - *A river bubbling over rocks.*
    - *My cat purring.*
    - *My friend playing Schubert on her elegant grand piano.*
    - *My husband saying, "After all these years, I still love you."*

3. Taste
    - *My first cup of steaming coffee in the morning.*
    - *Fresh fruit, strawberries, pineapple, raspberries.*
    - *A handful of salted mixed nuts.*
    - *A bowl of hot, nourishing homemade soup on a cold winter day.*
    - *A chocolate-dipped vanilla ice cream cone from Dairy Queen.*

4. Smell

- *Bread baking in the oven*
- *Bacon being fried (I don't eat it very often, but I love the smell).*
- *Freshly cut grass*
- *Essential oils simmering in my diffuser, especially lavender.*
- *Clean sheets that have been dried on the line outdoors.*

5. Touch
   - *The feel of soft, smooth sheets after a long day.*
   - *Patting my cat.*
   - *Warm hugs from family and friends.*
   - *The wind on my cheeks on a warm summer day.*
   - *Having a reflexology treatment.*

You don't need to stop with the five senses. Go on to name places, things, people, and activities that nourish you and fill you with joy.

Each of the things you have written down is like a little burst of joy in your day. The sensation may last only a few seconds, but the effects are long-lasting. After making your lists, try and incorporate as many of these "joy bursts" into your daily life as you possibly can. Remember: You are making deposits on the positive side of your "life bank account!"

6. Let it Go

At any point during the day when you realize that you are ruminating about negative thoughts, you can simply say quietly to yourself, "Let it go!" (Or if you are alone, it is even more effective to say it out loud!) This is a nonjudgmental way of releasing thought patterns that don't serve you. Perhaps you have been cut off in traffic, maybe you are angry about what someone said or did. It is totally natural for you to start allowing self-defeating thoughts to swirl around in your mind. Thoughts of revenge or frustration can begin festering like a suppurating wound. Maybe you are experiencing feelings of crippling anxiety that threaten to overwhelm you. The first step is to become aware of what is happening. Catch yourself, stop yourself in your tracks, and gently, but firmly, say the words, "Let it go." You can do this as many times as you need throughout the day. It is amazing to realize what a relief it is not to be enslaved by unwanted thoughts or judgments.

Letting go is a very effective strategy for dealing with things in the heat of the moment; however, you can apply it to a situation that has become entrenched in your life over the years, as well. Some people find themselves hanging onto grudges, disappointment, and resentment about events that occurred many years previously. I know of people who cling to feelings of anger, even hatred, for years. Why don't you take a moment right now and ask yourself if you are polluting your present well-being with mental garbage from the past. What negativity are you holding onto in your life? It is possible that you have held these negative thoughts for so long that they have become part of the wallpaper in your mind. You may not even be conscious of their existence. The act of letting go is a gentle, cleansing action that releases you from a past that has no business in the present.

The second half of letting go is an act of self-acceptance and exoneration. At any point, after you have let go of an intrusive thought or attitude, you can add the phrase, "Just start over." It's like turning the pages of a notebook to reveal a new blank page. You can begin anew. Like a book with many chapters, there are numerous new beginnings in your story.

Your future possibilities do not need to be limited by past failures.

Letting go and starting over are two ways that you can use, over and over, to make a new beginning.

PART THREE:
Some Specific Suggestions For Prevention and Care of Postpartum Depression

1. Education and Awareness

Although many efforts have been made to create more public awareness, postpartum depression remains a topic that is not adequately discussed among health practitioners or in the general public. Women who have had the very frightening experience of going through postpartum depression need to have their voices heard. We need to speak up and educate new mothers on the very real risks of developing postpartum depression after the birth of their baby. Prenatal classes and prenatal doctors' visits are the logical place to start with this education.

The education needs to focus on realistic expectations after giving birth. Experiencing a form of what is often called "baby blues" is a normal part of being a new mother. The exhausting labour process, sleepless nights, and hormonal fluctuations all contribute to feelings that are somewhat melancholic. It is not uncommon for new mothers to suddenly burst into tears for no apparent reason.

Postpartum depression is much more severe and unrelenting. It doesn't go away, even after getting a full night's rest. Its onset can be precipitous, as in my case, or it can come months after the birth of a baby. The most important thing you can do if you think that you might be having symptoms of postpartum depression is to reach out to someone you trust. Hopefully, your family doctor is well versed in the symptoms and can provide helpful advice and treatment.

2. Funding for Public Health Home Visits

It is my opinion that every new mother be paid a home visit by a knowledgeable and caring professional. It used to be that our government provided funding for public health nurses to visit new mothers in their homes. These visits focused mainly on the infant's nutrition, growth, and development, but could also have been used to screen the mother's overall health and emotional well-being—a vital missed opportunity. So often, I have heard it said that existing programs do not address mothers' needs. A mother's well-being often slips unnoticed between the cracks in our medical system. Preventive wellness programs are sadly lacking in our modern health-care system. The short-sightedness of cutting funding for these valuable supports has repercussions down the road. In other words, money that could have been used for early detection and prevention of postpartum depression is subsequently required to treat the unnecessary suffering of the women involved.

3. Know the Risk Factors

One of the most significant determinants of developing postpartum depression is previous experience with it. In addition, if there are any concurrent major stressors, such as a death in the family, a move, or an ill family member, the woman will be at greater risk. It is also imperative that healthcare professionals, as well as the individuals themselves, be cognizant of their mental-health history. If there is a record of any type of mental illness in the past—such as depression, anxiety, borderline personality disorder, or PTSD—the risk of developing postpartum depression is magnified.

4. Recognize the Existing Social Stigma

New mothers are expected to be happy and coping well with the experience of motherhood. As a result, women are reluctant to admit that they are having dark feelings and are overwhelmed with their role. This results in lack of support or isolation because mothers don't believe it is acceptable to state their true feelings.

5. Medical Follow-up

Ideally, doctors who are in the business of delivering babies should recognize mothers who present as high risk for postpartum depression. Despite the fact that my previous experience of postpartum depression was clearly documented in my obstetrical history, not one medical professional asked about my emotional well-being. This falls into the category of "things I need to let go of." Although I am not in the habit of ruminating about this part of my experience, it does feel rather unbelievable to think of how much suffering this oversight caused me and my family.

Medical professionals who conduct well baby visits have an even greater responsibility in the early detection of postpartum depression. It is imperative that mother and baby be considered as a single unit of care. A mother-newborn relationship is greatly symbiotic in nature. If the mother is suffering, the baby will also be at greater risk.

The only way of detecting the state of the mother's mental health is to ask direct, probing questions. Most mothers will do what is socially expected of them and say that they are fine. I highly recommend the use of the Edinburgh Depression Scale (Edinburgh Postnatal Depression Scale). It was originally developed in Britain and is one of the most widely used screening instruments for assessing symptoms of postpartum depression and anxiety. I believe that by using a scale such as this, health professionals could detect the early warning signs of women at risk and help them to seek the assistance that could prevent a full-blown postpartum depression. A PDF of the scale can be found at the following web page:

http://www.beyondtheblues.info/Docs/edinburgh%20english.pdf.

6. Friends and Partners Can Help

Partners of new mothers need to be fully aware of the stress and burden that motherhood places on women. Taking care of the needs of a newborn is a 24-7 task. Breastfeeding can be an exhausting, all-consuming endeavour. At a time when the need for excellent nutrition is paramount, a new mother often lacks the time or energy to prepare proper meals. Partners need to recognize that their emotional and practical support can make the difference between a mother's ability to cope and her descent into depression.

Friends can help by bringing home-cooked meals or offering to assist with household chores. Most importantly, the mother needs to feel safe enough to share her true feelings, no matter how conflicted they may sound. Partners and friends can support her process by listening in an empathetic, non-judgmental manner.

Partners and friends need to keep their eyes and ears open to recognize: a) signs of distress; and, b) the mother's inability to cope. They need to step up and advocate getting the mother professional help at this crucial time.

⚜

Building resilience is a lifelong process. It doesn't matter how often you get knocked down in life, as long as you keep getting up every time. At any given moment you have the power to say, "This is not how the story is going to end."

Acknowledgements

Even though they are no longer with us, I owe everything to my parents who brought me into this world and raised me with solid faith and values. I attribute my strong work ethic and integrity to my Dad's unfailing energy and enthusiasm. My mother taught me that nothing is more important than compassion for others, especially those who are hurting.

It goes without saying that I am the person I am today in large part because of my siblings who loved and teased me into adulthood. I am forever grateful for your love and shining example.

My 3 children, Hailey, Brandon and Alana: Thank you for the honor and privilege of being your mother. Please know that I will only ever be in one of 3 places: In front of you to cheer you on, behind you to have your back, or next to you so you aren't walking alone.

Bruce, you are my rock. You're my favorite place to go when my heart searches for reassurance and strength. Thank you for supporting me in the telling of my story.

Thank you to Ellen who agreed to give my manuscript a "first-pass" and provided encouraging and helpful feedback.

Thank you to Jocelyn who wholeheartedly supported my project and gave me her thumbs up "go girl!" endorsement.

Thank you Dr. Graham. You were there for me when my world was broken.

Thank you to anyone who has been part of my journey of healing and resilience. You know who you are and even though I have not mentioned you by name, your love and support have helped bring me to where I am today.

CPSIA information can be obtained
at www.ICGtesting.com
Printed in the USA
LVHW071033080919
630099LV00003B/2/P

9 781525 541155